Chance
or
Circumstance?

CHANCE
OR
CIRCUMSTANCE?

**A MEMOIR AND JOURNEY THROUGH THE STRUGGLE
FOR CIVIL RIGHTS REVISED EDITION**

James R. Mapp
Editors: Anthony Mapp, Brenda
Hackett, Michaellee Duckworth

CHANCE OR CIRCUMSTANCE?
A MEMOIR AND JOURNEY THROUGH THE STRUGGLE
FOR CIVIL RIGHTS REVISED EDITION

iUniverse books may be ordered through booksellers or by contacting:

iUniverse
1663 Liberty Drive
Bloomington, IN 47403
www.iuniverse.com
844-349-9409

ISBN: 978-1-6632-5666-9 (sc)
ISBN: 978-1-6632-5681-2 (e)

Library of Congress Control Number: 2023918968

Print information available on the last page.

iUniverse rev. date: 01/08/2024

In Loving Memory

JAMES R. MAPP

August 16, 1927 – June 19, 2015

CONTENTS

DEDICATION

To THE MEMORY OF MRS. VIOLA Mapp . . . my late wife of forty-six years and four months. Vi was the best companion a husband could have; the greatest mother children could hope for and a delight to her late parents and many siblings. She embodied the kind of love that never dies. As a mother of the civil rights movement, Vi was full of compassion and humanity, vision and foresight. She had a faith and commitment to the African American people of Chattanooga, Tennessee that was without peer. It is my hope and prayer that therein, Viola Martin Mapp will be a source of encouragement and inspiration to young women. And I hope that young men will seek mates with these ideals in mind.

This book is also dedicated to Bettye Jean McCoy-Mapp, my current wife, for her unending patience and understanding while I took on this endeavor. She has been patient, enduring some of my not-so-good days while constantly encouraging me. I have a special word of thanks to you.

I add a tribute to my own mother, Mrs. Mattie L. Davis, and Vi's mother, Mrs. Beatrice Martin as well as my niece Sandra Smith.

EPIGRAPH

"JAMES R. MAPP WAS ONE OF the great innovators in our city."

> The Honorable Andy Berke, Mayor, City of Chattanooga
> April 21, 2016, Rededication of the James R. Mapp
> Building at the University of Tennessee at Chattanooga.

"I was there during those dastardly days of the NAACP and it was not nice. My Dad was one of the men who had to carry shotguns at night to guard the community. They were threatening not only to kill the Mapps but everybody else."

> The Honorable Dr. Tommie Brown, Former Tennessee
> State Representative
> April 21, 2016, Rededication of the James R. Mapp
> Building at the University of Tennessee at Chattanooga

"The moral compass of the community, improving the lives of all of us. James R. Mapp dedicated his entire life to really serving others."

> Richard Brown, Executive Vice Chancellor for Finance-
> Operations and Information Technology, University of
> Tennessee at Chattanooga
> December 20, 2017, Dedication of James R. Mapp Street
> which intersects Martin Luther King Boulevard.

James R. Mapp had a favorite phrase, "We don't concern

ourselves with what others think when we know the thing that we must do is right." It may come as no surprise that Mapp was a walking history book and life resource. He identified with the poor and jobless because his family was forced to move from a Georgia sharecropping community due to of the greed of a local land baron on the eve of the Second World War. He knew the significance of education, and whether it was pushing for more African-American and minority educators or feeder schools, he felt education was the greatest equalizer in America. He was familiar with the inequalities and inequities in criminal justice, having himself waged a 26-year struggle to gain equal access for all schools.

Eric A. Atkins, (B.A., History: TSU '02; M.Ed., Secondary Education: UTC '2014;) and 2014 Recipient James R. Mapp Citizen of the Year
https://www.chattanoogan.com/2015/6/25/30 3123/Mapp-s-History-Lesson--Stand-For-What.aspx

ACKNOWLEDGEMENTS

There are many who, at various times and in many ways, contributed to the work chronicled in this book. Thanks to Mr. Norvel Horton, Mrs. Doris Johnson Phipps, Ms. Beverly Scott, Mrs. Rose Martin and the late Dr. Barbara Medley (my right arm, editor and encourager). I wish to especially thank the late Robert L. J. Spence, his wife, and his son.

A special tribute to all our children, many of whom played an integral role with us in the Chattanooga civil rights struggle. No finer group of children, they, like me, loved and revered their mother. They are Brenda V. Hackett, DeBora L'T. Mapp-Embry, Michaellee M. Duckworth, James J. (Jon) Mapp, Angela M. Fritts, Herbert A. (Toney) Mapp, Alicia V. Mapp and Ivanetta D. (Ivy) Barksdale.

PREFACE

THE 1960S WERE A TIME WHEN the country had finally come face-to-face with de jure (legalized) and de facto (the common acceptance of) segregation. As a result, sit-in demonstrations across the south by high school and college students were occurring daily to protest the Jim Crow laws that made them second class citizens.

In Chattanooga, our demands for civil rights took place within the context of this national movement. My wife, Viola, and I along with Josephine Maxey and the Reverend H.H. Kirnon decided to once-and-for-all challenge the Chattanooga Board of Education's segregation policies. We demanded that local and state courts enforce rulings that through *Brown versus the Board of Education* had become national law six years earlier.

This book is historical, autobiographical and event oriented as it chronicles the civil rights movement of the 1960s in the city of Chattanooga, Tennessee. Many noteworthy happenings in the African American community have gone unrecorded. The heart of "Chance or Circumstance?" tells the century-old struggle for racial equality. The language used within describes African Americans as "colored, "Negro", or "Black". The change in terminology reflects the struggle for identity of a once enslaved people stripped of their true lineage and roots.

Chattanooga's civil rights struggle was rarely mentioned in the national press. Better known places such as Little Rock, Birmingham, Selma and Montgomery caught the national attention. However, the price paid and punishment inflicted for speaking out – demanding what is ours – remained the same for all.

As we keep the faith and work to eradicate racism, we must never forget there are no permanent friends or permanent enemies in politics, just permanent interests.

To the students, organizations and ordinary citizens of Chattanooga: over the years you found the nerve and conviction to join the attack on racial segregation. I applaud you. Without your commitment, so many victories would have not been possible. Your resistance yielded a changed city. A changed Chattanooga.

Progress-Regress-Progress

Right after the end of the civil war, across the south, a large-scale social revolution known as Reconstruction had occurred. For eight short years, once enslaved Negroes were suddenly doused with newfound rights and freedoms. Under the protection of the Union Army, Black men could now vote and hold elective office, thus redefining the politics of the region. In Chattanooga, Blacks were elected to positions as aldermen and constables and became full-fledged officers of the police force.

But the gradual return of southern states to the Union and Northern fatigue systematically eroded black political power and freedoms.

It would be another eight decades before enough momentum had been built up to attack en force the racial discrimination and segregation that took the place of slavery. During that time, while no longer the enslaved, one would be hard pressed to say that Black people were indeed "free".

This struggle for civil rights has never been a smooth or continuous effort. Rather it has come in fits and starts, success and regress with brief moments of light followed by long enduring darkness. In the context of this book, I present to the reader a civil rights family along with a handful of Chattanooga's black community who voluntarily stood squarely in the midst of racial conflict and public danger.

Cloaked only in the belief that our civil and equal rights are worth whatever sacrifice was demanded of us, we knew that only WE could master our own fate.

As I look back, I marvel at both the simplicity and complexity of my life. When starting married life in Chattanooga with Vi, my goal was simply be a faithful husband, father and provider. When it came to matters of the surrounding community, my life became increasingly complex as I juggled the roles of civic leadership and responsibility. As I now look in the rear-view mirror, some fifty years later, I'm in wonder how it all was accomplished.

All I knew was that our freedom can't be left up to others. And as so much was left up to us, I can't help but wonder how much assistance was contributed by the hand of the Divine. Was it all by *Chance or Circumstance*? This is my story as told in my own words.

CHAPTER 1

Thunder over Chattanooga

FEBRUARY 19, 1960 WAS A VERY pleasant day in Chattanooga, with no threat of rain or snow. Despite these ideal conditions, two symbolic claps of thunder were heard throughout the community due to two separate but related incidents.

The first clap that reverberated through the community occurred at Glenwood Elementary School about one thirty in the afternoon. I, along with our two children, Deborah and James, three other parents and their three children marched up the walkway to the all-white school in an attempt to desegregate. We parents agreed on day and time to act and were hopeful that success would occur in short order.

Nearby Orchard Knob Elementary, which was all Black, was so badly overcrowded that our students were being bussed out to three other locations for half-day sessions.

Within a few hours on the same day, a group of Howard High students were in the library for study hour. Among themselves they discussed the recent actions taken by black college students who had staged sit-ins to desegregate the lunch counters of Greensboro, North Carolina. Between them they wondered if any around the table had the nerve to pull off such a stunt. In typical teenage fashion, this question eventually led to a dare. Each challenged the other to go to the downtown business district and sit-in at the S. H. Kress lunch counter. All students knew it was against the law for them to sit at the same counter with whites, but with the simple act of just sitting, they reasoned what real harm could it do? They guessed they might be subject to harassment or even the outside chance of arrest, but they pressed on anyway. That's when the second *clap of thunder* rattled the city. Little did these Howard High School students know at the time that their actions would set in motion the beginning of active protests destined to change that sleepy southern city forever.

I often wondered if the two related, but unrelated events of that day were a result of chance or circumstance. I suppose arguments can be made for both, but I'd like to believe that not one, but two claps were God's way of not allowing us to second guess ourselves. If one incident didn't have the power to collectively move us, then two left little question of the path we were to take. At any rate . . . What a day!

DESEGREGATING CHATTANOOGA SCHOOLS

Members of the Negro Parent Teach Association (PTA) had frequently complained about the conditions of our children's schools, equipment, and books. As parents, we simply wanted a complete day of education for our children and were willing to take on the system to see that it happened. Due to the city administration's stance toward segregation, no one really expected this seemingly tranquil community to be interrupted by a handful of disgruntled parents. The prevailing attitude was that Black and white citizens were satisfied with the current education system in place.

Chattanooga's NAACP (National Association for the Advancement of Colored People) Executive Committee had previously considered a proposal from the membership to file a school desegregation lawsuit. But, in the end they rejected the proposal for two reasons. First, it was thought that to even entertain such a notion, a war chest of at least $2,000 was required. The local branch was raising a sum of about $300 a year. Secondly, the executive committee thought there should be a survey of the entire city before a lawsuit is even considered.

Although the executive committee wasn't supportive, I, as president and other NAACP members wanted to move independently of the local branch. We had no idea how the committee would react and frankly, we didn't care. Our children were our top priority. The Supreme Court doctrine of "separate but equal" had never served us because there was never any real desire to create an equal playing field. To us, the executive committee was foolish to trust that the school board would do the right thing. Past history told us all we needed to know. So, we proceeded on and started making plans.

You can imagine the shock when negro parents and students appeared out of the blue at the all-white elementary school. The principal immediately took us to her office. She was flustered but retained self-control as she informed us in no uncertain terms that she had no authority to admit our children. The board of education had not changed its policy of racial separation.

Undeterred, we left the school and went to the NAACP office to promptly send Dr. Letson, the school superintendent, a telegram demanding that the school system be desegregated within twenty-four hours. We also called the national NAACP and requested they intervene on our behalf. In no time our demands hit the local grapevine. Over the entire city, white parents and students alike were filled with confusion, apprehension, anger, and fear. But the die had been cast, and there was no turning back.

We wanted to file a lawsuit to desegregate the schools and asked the national office of the NAACP for their support. They accepted our request. On April 6, 1960, Attorney Constance Baker Motley arrived from New York. Attorney Motley, who would later become a federal judge, was directed to act in quick order. She kidded us about the audacity of our twenty-four-hour demand as she filed the lawsuit, assisted by R.H. Craig a local attorney.

Before Attorney Motley's arrival, the word around was there was nothing to worry about. The local branch of the NAACP had not approved the suit. But when Attorney Motley stepped off the plane at Lovell Field, it was a great shock to Black leaders who had already given their word to the white establishment that nothing was going to happen. It wasn't long before a delegation of upset parents called on me. I thought it inconceivable that their immediate concern wasn't for their children but rather their focus to get someone Black on the school board.

Negroes Ask Integration Within City
In District Court: Suit Against School Board Brought by Parents of 4 Children. **Integration Suit Filed on Schools:** Parents Seek 5-Part Relief Against Operation of Biracial System. A lawsuit asking the federal courts to order city authorities to desegregate the Chattanooga public school system was initiated this Wednesday in the U.S. district court... R.H. Craig, a Chattanooga attorney, filed the suit. He has attorneys from other parts of the country, two of them with national stature, associated in the case. They are Thurgood Marshall and an associate in his New York law firm, Constance Baker Motley, and Z. Alexander Looby and Avon Williams, Nashville attorneys. *Chattanooga Daily Times* archives, April 7, 1960.

Members of the local Executive Committee, including Rev. Dr. Major Jones, the Reverend Horace Tyler, the Reverend H.H. Battle (who would later become the first black to serve on the Board of Education), asked me to withdraw the lawsuit. I told them "No". At this point Dr. Jones, a close associate of Dr. Martin Luther King threatened, "If you do not withdraw this suit, you may as well fold up the NAACP charter and send it back to New York".

It was apparent that the Black leadership had already struck some sort of deal. They trusted that in the long run the white community would do the "right thing" as long as we didn't press too hard or "rock the boat". It was hard to believe that our children's fate was subject to such backroom politics. For whatever reason, the black leadership of Chattanooga was content to allow the white man in his own sweet time to "hand us" our equality as if it was a gift instead of a right. To those of us calling for immediate change, this was just one more effort to find some way around mixing of the races. And sadly, the so-called Black leadership of Chattanooga was falling for it.

DESEGREGATING THE LUNCH COUNTERS

Howard High school students were inspired by the sit-in protests that occurred in Nashville Tennessee just ten days earlier. They also were aware that college students in other cities were organizing as well. In Chattanooga, the youth now felt it was their turn to act.

The students entered the S.H. Kress five and dime store on Market Street at four in the afternoon. As they drifted in, some admitted they were about to lose their nerve and turn around. Their courage was suddenly bolstered when they saw their classmate, Melvin Davis, go directly to and seat himself at the lunch counter. One by one the students followed, making good the dare that led them there. If counter service had been given, I wondered if they'd even have the money to pay. Nevertheless, they stayed put, making history as Rosa Parks did a few years earlier "standing up" for their rights, by "sitting down".

Before then, Black people had to stand in a small corner of the dining area to eat food they had purchased. More oft than not, they simply paid for their order and left. If they stayed, they could only look on as white people sat and sneered at the "coloreds". Each student who sat down that day knew it was possible they might be confronted by the police. But none were aware that to be caught sitting at the lunch counter was also a felony. Jim Crow laws were to be obeyed and not challenged.

When Melvin and the others sat, the waitress didn't serve them. Instead, the manager called the police, and the students were promptly arrested and jailed. After hearing of the arrests, their parents called on the local branch of the NAACP and as president I immediately started the process of engaging legal counsel to facilitate their release.

Negroes "Sit Down Here"; No Incident, No Service
Group carries out Protest in Downtown Chattanooga Store.
Chattanooga Daily Times archives, February 20, 1960.

The efforts of these brave students shocked the city and signaled there was no turning back. Word of Friday's activity electrified the Black community and on the following Monday more students joined in the protest. By February 22nd an organization had been formed under the leadership of Paul Walker, president of the Howard High senior class. He and other students formed a liaison with the local NAACP, and it was agreed that as the demonstrations continued, they would keep the branch abreast of all plans and actions.

After the first sit-ins, Dr. James Lawson, a Methodist minister and a member of the Southern Christian Leadership Conference (SCLC), began teaching the students proven non-violent techniques. He mainly focused on training them to not react – no matter the circumstances. He included exercises to ready them mentally for the ramped-up abuse surely to come their way.

The students originally met at St. Mary's, a quaint little brown framed church, but the crowd that gathered soon grew too large, prompting the much larger First Congregational Church to open its doors.

Day after day, the church was filled with eager participants. Students were divided into four separate groups. Four coordinators were chosen, one for each of the five-and-dime stores to be targeted. The thoughtful strategy and precision executed by the students was a testament to their growing discipline and determination. In their heart of hearts, they knew they were onto something. And they knew that because of their efforts, Chattanooga's Black folk finally had Mister Jim Crow on the run.

When it came to supporting the student's cause, St. Mary's and the First Congregational Church were the exception within the Black church community. Although the church is universally thought of as the backbone of the national civil rights movement, in Chattanooga most black churches were reticent in their support. Others just downright refused to weigh in. Their silence was deafening and noticed. I feared the mixed messages of support and non-support might provide hope to those who thought that progress could still be halted due to the lack of common consensus.

As student after student sat at the lunch counter, their eyes were cast downward, their hands deliberately clasped. These efforts helped to keep in check any basic instinct to protect themselves by raising their arms or fists. During the encounter they endured insults, thrown food and drink, cigarette burns, and the most hateful stares white racists could manage to conjure.

About 200 Negroes in Sitdowns at Four Stores
The lunch counter sitdown launched here Friday by students from Howard High School was resumed Monday with a larger number who occupied four Market Street variety store counters. *Chattanooga Daily Times* archives, February 23, 1960.

Day after day there were arrests. The many students participating in the "sit-ins" and later the "stand-ins" were locked up in record numbers. Older students were sent to jail and had to have bail posted. Those seventeen and under were paraded before the juvenile court and released to the custody of their parents.

Parents of the students in the initial protest had no idea their children would take it upon themselves to meddle in what was considered "grown folk business". They had drilled into their kids from a very young age, obeyance of the law – whatever it might be – as a matter of self-preservation. Black parent's greatest fear was that such flouting of regulations could put their kids' future in jeopardy or even cause the unbearable – the loss of their lives. Parents also were aware that due to their children's actions, it was very possible that their own jobs might hang in the balance.

As president of the local branch of the NAACP, I retained lawyer Craig to defend the students. I also called on our treasurer, Dr. James Bynes, to bail out those arrested. As the sit-ins continued, even the Black leadership, who first opposed the very idea, became believers. Among their ranks, some quietly put up bail money for the students.

East Ninth Street (now Martin Luther King Jr. Boulevard) was a predominantly Black business district and a safe haven for the students. Business owners and workers were "prepared" should violence erupt along that downtown corridor. They had weapons of all kinds and some boldly advertised that fact. From the barber to the liquor store owner to the fellas hanging on the corner, it was understood and went without saying that our students would be protected at all costs.

Once the protests started, some nonstudents armed themselves and attempted to join in. They were promptly rejected because their intentions didn't represent the spirit of non-violence. Our students had internalized the lessons of peaceful occupation. They truly believed in their cause. They trained their minds to fight against the instinct to lash out. Such a commitment to peaceful protests converted naysayers who were originally convinced that a black violent uprising would be the only way to deal with what they called "this desegregation madness".

While the demonstrations were going on, white students from private schools were instructed not to venture downtown. Those who ignored the warnings were called in by their principals and temporarily suspended. As most were curious onlookers, there were those "true believers" among them who wanted the status quo to continue. On both sides, those eager to incite were the ones authorities mostly kept their eye on. Any hint of violence by either side would guarantee to make already bad matters worse.

From the beginning of the lunch counter revolt, Black teachers and administrators were fearful of what might happen. But as the protests wore on, their deep resentment of the one-sided education system broke to the surface of their consciousness and some became secret under-the-table supporters.

The superintendent of schools ordered the Black principals to dissuade their students from protesting, but to no avail. The principals even threated to "tell your momma" as if that were the ultimate peril. Their intimidations meant very little to fast maturing students who by now had endured "trials by fire".

In unusually cold weather in March of 1960, the authorities tried to stop the students from gathering outside by turning fire hoses on them. No matter – the protesters persisted. Let me note that this occurred a full three years before Bull Conner, Montgomery Alabama's safety commissioner, made national news by turning fire hoses on their Black children.

Fire Hoses Curb Milling Crowd, Negroes Turned Off Market; Cool Heads
Prevent Big Blow Up Hoses do not differentiate between trouble-makers
and bystanders [photo caption]. 20 Are Arrested: Seven Juveniles Are
Among the 11 Negroes and 9 Whites Seized ... Some Bottles Are Tossed
at Cars, but Violence in Isolated Incidents. Second Time for City to Use
Hose on Crowd. *Chattanooga Daily Times* archives, February 25, 1960.

To a growing number of Chattanoogans the firehose incident
was a shameful act performed against defenseless children. As
punishment, some claimed that the wrath of God was upon us
because in the days that followed a very unusual late winter ice
storm paralyzed the city. Wet and dreary, a general freeze had set
in. Lookout Mountain, where the "powers that be" resided, looked
like a dirty sheet of ice in the glare of the morning sun. Because
of the freeze, no one was able to go up or down the mountain for
two weeks running.

On May 13, 1960, about fifty students were arrested and put
under a one-hundred-dollar bond each. All but eight refused to
be released in the custody of our attorney. Instead, they chose to
stay in jail overnight. Those who refused bond certainly made the

point that they were determined to show that even jail could not deter them.

The initial sit-in involved only S.H. Kress & Company, but soon the protest spread to the lunch counters of F.W. Woolworth, McLellan's and W.T. Grant. This would continue in Chattanooga until all lunch counters were eventually opened and desegregated by December of 1960.

Around August of 1960, the students expanded their vision and set their sights on desegregating the downtown movie houses. They began picketing in February of the next year, and after some months of stand-in activity, the movie houses were desegregated. I found out in later years that some white youth would buy tickets and give them to the protesting students so that they could enter the movie houses.

Some thought that continued demonstrations alone were the answer. They also thought that the NAACP leadership coming to the bargaining table with city officials and others was a compromise. The Chattanooga branch of the NAACP and I were criticized even though the local branch had paid for most of the bonds and all of the legal fees. We were also criticized because we welcomed leadership from the mayor's office who supported our position.

It was said that there came much soul searching within the leadership of the city to the point that some hearts did soften, prompting a dialogue to seek solutions.

Mayor Pete Olgiati was regarded as the leader who helped shape the modern blueprint of Chattanooga, Tennessee. A political pragmatist, he eventually saw the handwriting on the wall and realized that these protests were not going to subside until real change was won. In an effort to move things forward, Mayor Pete removed the city attorney from the pro segregation school board. It would still be months before the mayor favored opening schools to all. The mayor didn't want to drain city coffers by spending taxpayer money in what was already decreed by the U.S. Supreme Court. The three-time mayor would lose his re-election race in 1963. It was thought that his concessions over desegregation contributed to his loss.

As the students had been in the struggle for some time now, there rose a renewed determination to finish the fight. Parents, at first reluctant were won over by the heroics of their children brave enough to place their hand in the lion's mouth of controversy.

The Howard High students would have had felonies on their records had not Attorney R.H. Craig petitioned to have the felonies expunged. He also arranged it so that arrested students never had to personally appear in court.

Up in age and from an earlier generation, Attorney Craig was slender, dark in complexion and very stately. He was one of two black attorneys in the city at the time. When talking to a judge he might say *boss* or words to that effect, which were used by many Negro lawyers. He was by no means considered an Uncle Tom as he negotiated and used his wily skills when dealing with those in the white community.

The fact that Attorney Craig lived in East Chattanooga in the area that we called KKK headquarters illustrates the kind of bravery he possessed. Even the staunch segregationist, county Judge Raulston Schoolfield, had great respect for him.

Attorney Craig diligently handled all the cases while he was suffering from cancer that would eventually prove fatal. As his health declined, I would often go by his office to talk and shave his face. Just before he succumbed to cancer, he pointed his long finger at me and said "Mr. Mapp, I have had the felonies of the sit-in and stand-in students expunged from the record. The NAACP owes me nothing. This is my gift to the young people".

Because the students did not have felonies, they were able to pursue professional and other ventures awaiting their futures. The students did not know of Attorney Craig's gift until I divulged it to them years later. Some went into jobs where top security clearance was necessary, such as the Secret Service and the Tennessee Valley Authority (TVA). Attorney Craig's commitment was quite a contrast to today's black attorneys who are often reluctant to take on civil rights cases even when fees are not a problem. Upon Attorney Craig's death, Attorney Bruce Boynton stepped in and represented us locally in the school desegregation suit.

We were blessed that in all that time violent confrontation did not occur in Chattanooga, even though there was a good chance that full scale riots could have erupted. As the protesting Howard High students prepared for college and other ventures, the power and spirit of non-violence remained in their hearts and minds.

CHAPTER 2
The Power of Direct Action

The Power of Direct Action

It appears that the happenings of February 19, 1960, must be termed as direct action first by adults and secondly by Howard students. I don't recall any individual or group taking to the source of trouble en masse prior to this day in Chattanooga. These were times of frustration and had been for a very long time with no individual or group willing to move on the sources of our problems. Both groups were motivated to seek improvement of the conditions that we were living under in Chattanooga.

–Excerpt from editorial written by James R. Mapp

THE DIRECT ACTIONS OF THE SIT-INS, stand-ins and challenges to desegregate schools gave an immediacy to our problems as we sought to expose institutions that had long kept Blacks as second-class citizens. Black Chattanooga had finally galvanized enough to collectively begin challenging the integrity of the courts, the police and education departments, as well as the business community. It was time for Chattanooga's long held "laissez-faire" (or leave alone) attitude to be addressed when it came to the daily mistreatment and degradation of African American people.

14

Although so-called "free" after a bitter Civil War, with the exception of a few short years during Reconstruction where the formally enslaved were protected by union soldiers enforcing the peace, there was no such thing as Black people of Chattanooga enjoying full benefits of citizenry. Once reconstruction ended and the troops were withdrawn, revenge and violence was perpetrated with impunity, Black women were expected to present themselves with heads bowed in the most subservient of ways. Black men were to be submissive to all white males, no matter their station or age or competence-simply for having white skin was the key to having the backing of every available level of power.

Our status as a worthy people was non-existent in a society that had the full support and backing of the segregationist powers. This being the case meant that the wholesale daily surrender of our basic humanity was the price we dearly paid so we could provide for our families, maintain the lowliest of jobs or steer clear or the law. Mind you, punishment could easily be inflicted as a result of the flimsiest white accusation.

The dual actions in the first steps of our liberation that took place on that February day in 1960 injected true feelings of hope as we took our first steps wading into the "waters of freedom". Over the next few months, despite all of the unknowns, we dared to venture deeper and deeper. Nervous but determined, we moved forward, each step further from the shores of servitude while being mindful of the uncertainty that could surely overtake and drown us.

Little did we realize that the actions to desegregate the local lunch counters and other public and business spaces would be accomplished in a relatively short period of time as compared to the twenty-six-year court battle to fully desegregate Chattanooga's schools.

Taking the segregation issue head on, in 1963 newly elected mayor Ralph Kelley (Who later became a federal judge) formed a ten-member Bi-Racial Committee. Five whites and five blacks were tasked to give the leadership to solve the dilemma of desegregating Chattanooga. On September 24, 1963 Mayor Kelley declared city facilities "open to all". This included public buildings, parks, playgrounds, swimming pools, golf courses and community centers.

One great irony is that this was same Ralph Kelley who two years earlier as a state legislator helped pass the Barratry Law specifically designed to curb the activities of individuals and civil rights groups like the NAACP. It was also ironic that he had unseated three-time incumbent Mayor Olgiati because many white Chattanoogans felt that when it came to desegregation, Olgiati had been too willing to compromise

The bi-racial committee sought to bring the image of Chattanooga into a more positive light. It also moved to make substantial changes in the less than equal conditions that existed citywide. All in all, the committee made great progress in addressing the demands of all concerned.

Despite the ongoing progress, stories in the *Chattanooga Times* and *Chattanooga News Free Press* still endeavored to exploit old racial tensions. Their editorials sought to maintain the status quo by stirring anger and resentment within the white community. But this strategy wouldn't be as effective as it had been in the past because of the Bi-Racial committee there was a broad mix of local influencers including me. We all genuinely wanted to help curtail the animosity ginned-up by race baiting publications.

One soft-spoken member of the committee was businessman Felix Miller, one of the biggest advertisers in the Chattanooga dailies. Mr. Miller assumed the key role of obtaining valued leverage by getting the papers to tone down their rhetoric. Mr. Miller tried to live what he now preached and in doing so, became one of the first major employers in the city to upgrade black employee jobs and pay.

Felix Miller was very adept in making the editorial boards "see the light". He would calmly push Roy McDonald (publisher of the Chattanooga News Free Press) to tone down the divisive rhetoric and accept the inevitable change. McDonald, a segregationist son of the South took a bit of convincing but would eventually bow to the influence of "green power". When all was said and done it was the desire to hold onto the almighty dollar that eventually changed minds.

In later years, McDonald would host real estate agents at his farm. This included black guests. The hospitality given by his family to this mixed group was more than one could imagine, given his prevailing attitude. And although he "played the integration game" when it came to matters financial—throughout his career - McDonald stubbornly clung to his separatist views until the end of his days. Business dictated he keep a courteous veneer, but in his heart of heart refused to change with evolving attitudes and times.

On the other hand, one-time segregationist Mayor Ralph Kelley became a true believer in the benefits of integration. He took pride in saying that his leadership helped keep the societal problems in his fair city off the front pages of the New York Times. So whole heartedly he believed in inclusion that at the time of his death Judge Kelley became one of the few white people who would have his funeral arrangements done by the Franklin Strickland Funeral Home, a black-owned mortuary. In Chattanooga this was unheard of.

Here were two white men from similar backgrounds and accomplishments, struggling with the same moral issues of the day. In the end, one finds personal and political benefit by casting out practices of the past, while the other superficially changes due to matters of business. It is hard to figure the rationale of people who have every advantage and claim superiority by keeping their foot on the neck of others. To me...what shapes their perspective is not strength but fear.

The Bi-Racial Committee eventually overcame the initial skepticism of the Black community and gained respect as it labored to bring about changes. Even the Chattanooga Times began to take a more peaceful stance to calm the community. One reporter in particular named Springer Gibson worked to bring an objective mirror to reflect the cold hard facts of racist behavior the white community still clung to. Gibson's voice of reason, sensitivity and fairness was rare for a white journalist at that time. His even-handed reporting gave him an honored place in the history of racial reconciliation in the city.

The first strategy of the Bi-Racial committee was to integrate restaurants and other eating places in Chattanooga. The plan called for a number of Black and white adults to assemble on designated Saturday and spread out to restaurants city-wide. This demonstration was to prove that there was real change afoot and that all should be welcome to any business. A group and I and were assigned to eat breakfast at Bethea's Restaurant on Brainerd Road not far from my home. I had a good meal I must say that the management and help were very courteous. On that very encouraging day, all participants of our initial endeavor reported good treatment.

Because of the strong support of the mayor and the strength of the individuals on the Bi-Racial Committee Chattanoogans, especially Black Chattanoogans, began to hear that change was not only possible but real. The city was now open everyone. In 1964, the year following our great experiment, it was widely believed that the work of this Bi-Racial committee had a great deal to do with Chattanooga being honored and labeled an "All American City" by the National Civic League.

When it came to opening up entertainment venues and movie houses, protests by Howard High students had already softened management's resolve regarding integration. To leave no question as to the city's new policy, Mayor Kelley personally accompanied Black attorneys Bennie Harris, Bruce Boynton, and William T. Underwood to the Brainerd Theater.

With all intent and purpose, segregation of public spaces was in its last throes. This visible act by city officials all but finished it. In public spaces, the barriers that stood between Black and white Chattanooga had finally been torn down. But fully integrating the school system of Chattanooga, Tennessee was another matter indeed.

After four years I left the committee so that I could deal with other pressing NAACP related matters. Dr Luke Jackson, a Black dentist, replaced me. Buoyed by the success of the committee marked the point where I think the radical in me was, rekindled. In the school battle I knew I couldn't afford to be satisfied with our new gains. Change is never easy. Change...true change...real and lasting change has to be exercised and practiced every hour of every day of every week of every year. We can't afford to take our eye off the ball. Ever. I wondered if we Black folk in Chattanooga could maintain such discipline. Our progress was so fragile. So tentative. So much was still on the line. And I do believe that God helped us open the door, but He also left it up to us to find the determination and courage to keep it open.

CHAPTER 3
From Mayfield to Chattanooga

FROM EVERY CHILDHOOD THERE ARE MEMORIES that make deep impressions and have a lasting influence on who we are destined to be. Such experiences have contributed mightily to my own self-worth, morals and sense of fair play. I find myself lucky to have learned from the experience, generosity and wisdom of people around me. They helped me to become the person that I am today.

Early Years: I was born some five miles from a tiny town called Mayfield, Georgia on August 16, 1927. My mother was Mattie Lou Hargrove (Mapp) and my father was James Albert Mapp, a Baptist minister. Along with my younger sibling, Mary (whom we called Sister) we lived a typical hardscrabble existence among the pines of the mostly Black community which was no more than a few stone's throw from the railroad tracks.

I have but one memory of my father. He died in 1930 when I was three years old. The only lasting recollection was that one time he caught me climbing up the side of our hen house. He took me down and scolded me for bothering "them chickens". Once on the ground, I remember running after him around the little unpainted coop. The only picture I had of my father was placed in a Bible that somehow long ago got lost.

The memories of my father were so scant because according to Mother, he was a very possessive and jealous man. He was so unbearably jealous that when I was two years old Mother escaped with my sister and I to Chattanooga to live with her three brothers. I was two years old and Sister was only a few months old at the time. Although my mother was young – I was born when she was seventeen – she must have been in serious peril to uproot her two young children and leave her husband behind.

In pictures of her youth, Mother was indeed a beauty. She had an easy smile and laugh when she was amongst family. With strangers she was cautious and shy. Her light to medium brown complexion showed the blend of her ancestry. Mother had mostly African and native American roots. Her grandmother on her father's side was a full Cherokee, so we figured Mother was at least a quarter Indian. Her prominent cheekbones reinforced the idea of her native ancestry, and they were on full display when she smiled. Mother was considered tall for a woman of her time. Although gentle in demeanor, Mother was not one to suffer fools gladly. All her life she was a church-going woman and a child of the Holy Spirit. When it came to her children, she was very serious minded. With her there was little room for shenanigans and no room for lies. Mother held a strong but positive control over me and sister.

In 1930, while we were in Chattanooga, my father died due to complications from tuberculosis and pneumonia. With him no longer a menace, we moved back to Mayfield around 1933. We lived with Mother's sister, Aunt Rosa Tyus who had one son, Ned, who we called Junior. At one point we moved into a place called Raven Hill, where it was said that two spinsters had died in the house and that the house was haunted.

Mother was easy to scare, but Aunt Rosa wasn't afraid of anything. When Aunt Rosa was away, Mother piled sister and me in bed with her. On more that one occasion, we thought we saw ghosts at the foot of the bed and sometimes on the roof.

One day Mother sent me down the hill to the nearby spring. I was carrying a half gallon jar for water. While going down the hill I tripped and fell, breaking the jar. The glass cut the tendons in my right hand but the pockets on the bib overalls were thick enough to keep the broken glass from penetrating my chest. This happened just before the time I was to enter school. The serious wound threw me back one full academic year.

In 1935, searching for work and a new beginning, Mother moved back to Chattanooga. She left sister and me with my grandpa Henry Hargrove, a Baptist minister, and my grandma Elnora. During this time, I learned the workings of the farm and did chores daily: milking cows, feeding the hogs, chopping cotton, hoeing corn and anything else that was required. This was a time when farmers didn't want grass in their yards so as to keep away grazing animals and their leftovers from our shoes and feet. As part of my daily chores, I pulled up the small green tufts and swept the yard clean with a broom made out of dogwood branches.

One of the things I will remember not so fondly from those days was how I hated for the cows to break out of the fence in the wintertime. There was snow and ice I had to go into the woods to find them. Stupid cows!

On a typical southern farm in the country the meals were breakfast, dinner and supper. Dinner, the main meal of the day, was at noon. After one hour's rest we'd go back to the field, no matter how hot the Georgia sun was.

Grandma, the cook of the family fixed us real nice lunches for school. But now and again Grandpa would be in one of his peculiar moods – what we called "having his spell on" -where he insisted on fixing our lunches. Needless to say, those lunches wouldn't be anything like my grandmother's. Later on, I found out that Grandpa did the same thing to my mother, her sisters and brothers. I remember how they, now grownups, would laugh as they would recall stories of how bad the lunches were . . . so bad that they would hide their lunch buckets outside of the school and eat Grandpa's concoctions far away from the other students. We never knew why Grandpa would occasionally "have his spell on" . . . but I guess we all have some quirks of our own.

The first school we attended was a log cabin church that sat on stilts high above the ground. It was called Reynolds Grove. From time to time there were school affairs in the evening. Grandpa roasted and sold peanuts that were often half green, but people bought them anyway.

In 1990, I went to see my old school only to find that it and the nearby church were long gone. The only structure remaining was the log cabin, which was now being used as a tiny hunting lodge. The dirt road leading to the school was just as it was in 1937 when we left Georgia for the final time. As a kid, you couldn't tell me that this sandy road in the red hills of Georgia wasn't an important highway. But the single lane path, never much wider than a car, somehow shrank with time. It's funny how everything seems so much larger and important when you're young.

By the time I was nine, I was plowing the field with Ole Luedella, our horse. I was afraid when I came to the end of the row because it was then that I had to turn the horse around around and face her. I don't know why, but I had a fear of her looking directly at me.

My cousin, Ned, was a bit older and he would persuade me to do things that weren't necessarily in my best interest. Once Grandpa grew a prize melon and Ned convinced me to go to the field and get it. I picked the wrong one, so Ned sent me back again. As luck would have it, Grandpa caught us and gave both of us a whuppin.

As my cousin Ned grew into his teens, he developed the same nerves of steel as Aunt Rosa. Ned had no fear as he would go out into the blackness of the country night, a-courting some local girl. I'd often hear him whistling as he came down the dark country road, fearing nothing as he passed the graveyard, ignoring the barking and baying dogs along the way. I hoped some of his fearlessness would one day rub off on me.

One incident I vividly remember involved a trip to Gum Hill to visit my great grandparents. We rode in a Model- Ford. On the way, there was a steep hill that made the trip difficult. In order to make it, the car had to be backed up the hill. Everyone had to get out of the car so that all the males could push while the ladies walked. It took some time and plenty of effort, but we finally made it to the top.

Grandpa was pastor of a church. To get there he had to catch the train, ride a few miles and then walk the rest of the way. The story is that on one particular Sunday as he was making his way to catch the train home, a man picked him up in a buggy. The man never said a word as they rode along, and when they came to a certain fork in the road, the man motioned for Grandpa to get out. The next Sunday, Grandpa related to his church members how nice this man was who gave him a ride and how he never spoke a word. After telling the story, the astonished members gasped and told Grandpa it couldn't have been the fellow he described because that fellow had been killed earlier the same day on the road where he had turned off. "My Lord", Grandpa said, "that was the man"! I'm sure he puzzled over the strange occurrence for what I expect was the rest of his days.

Along with childhood remembrances came some of my life's most valued lessons. In 1937, Grandma and Grandpa finally retired from farming and were preparing to join their children in Chattanooga. But before they left, a local white man known as Mr. Little Arthur Reynolds (yes, that's what they called him) came around. He had caught wind that Grandpa was leaving and decided to seize upon the opportunity.

Mr. Little Arthur Reynolds told Grandpa flat out, "Henry, we are going to take the farm and call it even". Grandpa was stunned at the boldness and self-assuredness of the white man's claim. He replied, "But I don't owe you anything". Nevertheless, Mr. Little Arthur Reynolds insisted that there was indeed a debt owned. And in that part of the south, there was nothing a Colored man could say or prove that would supersede-even the most unsubstantiated-claim of any white man.

Back then, there was no need for Mr. Little Arthur Reynolds to provide proof. As a white man in middle Georgia, his say was proof enough. When Grandpa resisted, Mr. Little Arthur Reynolds raised his claim. He saw Ole Luedella, Grandpa's sixteen-year-old horse grazing nearby and stated, "We'll take the horse, too".

No matter how much Grandpa could prove there was no basis to Mr. Little Arthur's claim, there was no court to hear a case against a white man – and no lawyer to take such a case in the first place.

Although the actual words were never spoken, it was understood that in order for my grandparents, sister and me to achieve safe passage, Grandpa had no choice but to pay an "exit tax". Grandpa had no choice but to give up both the farm and the horse. Years later, Mother would tell me that such thievery ran in the family as Mr. Little Arthur Reynold's father, known as Mr. Big Arthur, did the same thing to another colored family. This lesson in inequity and powerlessness has followed me throughout my entire life. And given my life's path, I think it affected me more than I was ever aware.

On leaving for Chattanooga, we were taken to Crawfordville by Mr. Mark Jackson, one of the few Negroes in the region who had a car. We then caught a train about four in the morning. I remember wondering that although we never had a clock, we were somehow always on time.

Anyhow, those were days when we coloreds had to ride up front of the train. We sat nearest the black puffing steam engine and were subject to breathe the soot and fine coal dust that covered our clothes. In the front "colored" car I remember the smell of chicken fried in lard that filled the air. We didn't have cooking oils and shortening like we have today, so we used the lard (or pork fat) to fry foods. And the heavy odor of frying would cling to our clothing and smell up the whole coach.

When we arrived in Chattanooga, mother was remarried to a man named Will Davis. We lived in a three-room shotgun duplex on Blackford Street in a Negro neighborhood called Bushtown. I was happy to have a stepfather. At the time, Papa Will worked for a builder J. W. B. Lindsey and my mother worked as a maid for his wife in Red Bank. Mother worked seven days a week from Sunup until sundown, except Sundays when she got off early. Her weekly pay was $3 plus bus fare.

Our duplex got very cold in the winter and very hot in the summer. We had a fireplace where we burned wood and coal to keep warm. The wood came from waste at the construction sites where my stepfather worked and much of our coal came courtesy of the Southern Railroad Company - by way of the excess coal that fell to tracks from the open top cars. Some folks made a living by filling sacks with waste coal to sell. And a few bolder souls would actually sneak on top of the coal cars and throw off nuggets to make sure they'd have plenty to sell.

In 1937, Mother enrolled me and Sister in Orchard Knob Elementary School. When the school opened in 1902, it was originally named the 10th District School and housed grades one through 12. The name was changed to Orchard Knob Elementary in 1904. When we enrolled, I was supposed to be in the 4th grade. Mother went to take sister to the third grade and while she was gone, I upped and followed them to Mrs. Cox's third grade classroom. Mother told me to turn around and rejoin my class, but Mrs. Cox asked her to let me stay. Mother relented and as a result, I was now two grades behind where I should have been.

Looking back, I've learned that it doesn't take much to skew our individual timelines- setting us off on journeys we never knew we were supposed to take. It's the seemingly little acts of place and time and circumstance that alter our outlook and take hold of our minds. If I had gone to where I was "supposed to be" and followed all rules strictly and without question, would I have missed my destiny? Or did these random twists of fate shove me and my life into the space I was meant to occupy?

As I lived year after year there was little notice, but as I now look back and reflect on the overall map of my life (no pun intended) it's hard to argue – be it chance or circumstance, that my life was ultimately determined by God's Will, as a part of his master plan.

CHAPTER 4
Early Years in Bushtown

LIFE'S LESSONS

THE AREA OF CHATTANOOGA THAT WE lived was called Bushtown. The first morning we arrived I went out to the back porch and saw from a distance a freight train speeding by. "Mother, I said, "Look at that train! And I mean it's a-wailin' too". The year was 1937 and I was now ten years old. The fast-moving train excited me as I had been so used to the very slow locomotives full of stacked Georgia pine that by-passed sleepy little Mayfield. At that moment, just like the speeding train, I sensed that our livesspeeded up as well.

I soon met some of the boys and girls on our street and in our neighborhood. They called me by my nickname, "Buddy". There was Nat and Teatot, William, Eugene, Jeff, Richard and Virginia, Charles, Ruddy and later, another Charles. These Bushtown kids were the group of which I was mostly associated. We had some wonderful times playing in the streets and on vacant lots. But we had to be every mindful of our conduct because back then the entire neighborhood had eyes. One person in particular, Mrs. Ida Hunt, watched everything. Whether we were minding our own business or "acting up", Mrs. Hunt saw it as her duty to daily report our goings on to our parents.

Although Mrs. Hunt may have meant well, many a "whuppins"

were bestowed on members of our group depending on the degree she skewed her reports. Bushtown was one of those communities where "everybody knows everybody". And it wasn't unusual for neighbors to punish us kids with small swats or light smacks to the back of the head before they passed you along to your relatives for your final sentencing.

The last punishment my mother gave me was the result of a lie I told. Looking back, it was a simple matter. A group of us were supposed to go straight to the playground on Orchard Knob Avenue. On the way we got distracted by tadpoles swimming in a nearby branch that was lined with green slimy moss. For the better part of the afternoon we entertained ourselves with our new wiggly friends. Somehow or another, the slime along the bank made it from the water onto our clothes. Mother was at work so our neighbor, Mrs. Iva Spence was the one who would relate our adventure that day.

Once we grew tired of the tadpoles and headed home, we all knew we were in trouble. We contemplated on how to hide the green tell-tale evidence of not being where we were supposed to be in the first place. So we stopped by the old abandoned Lincoln High School, another "no-no" and thought it might be a good idea to cover up the evidence by rubbing sand onto our wet clothes. This only made matters worse. When Mrs. Spence saw the mess that was her son Jeff - to save his own hide – Jeff quickly spilled the beans. This became the official story Mother heard.

When mother asked me what happened, I gave her my version. She asked me again and I had already forgotten what I had told her the first time. Mother asked me for a third time, and along the way that story changed again. To get caught red-handed "tellin a tale" – us good little Christian kids weren't allowed to use the word "lie" – it guaranteed that you'd be directed to "go to the hedges, and bring back a switch" for a full-on whuppin.

Mother told me that she was not whuppin' me for what I had done but for not telling her the truth. From that day on, I never lied to her again. Mother was almost always proud of me and Sister. Back then folks didn't directly say the words "I love you" but we were smart enough to realize that her many sacrifices on behalf of Mary and me said it all.

When I was about eleven years old, there was an incident that really troubled and stuck with me over the years. One spring day, Richard Kelly and I went to Ben Magolin's Grocery store. Richard's mother had an account there. I went with him to pick up some items she had sent him to fetch. Once we were in the store, Richard saw that the owner was distracted so he quickly shoved a box of animal cookies in my hand and told me to head out of the store, which I did.

It happened so quickly that I didn't have time to think, but inside I immediately knew it was wrong. Nevertheless, I tightly tucked the cookies to my side and made my way out of the store to the sidewalk. I tried to tell myself that Richard must have put the cookies on his mother's bill, but I knew that wasn't the case.

I can't rightly remember if I ate the cookies or not, but I promised myself I'd never knowingly get caught in that kind of predicament again. Later, when I was older and worked in grocery stores, I made sure that the cost of anything I ate was carried on a list that would be deducted from my weekly paycheck.

In Bushtown, we kids enjoyed a very active life as we spent most of our time outside playing games and exploring our surroundings. We played I Spy, Hopscotch, Kick the Can and – depending on what kind of ball was available – engaged in pickup ball games. More oft that not we played with balls that were no more than knotted rags put in an old sock. Our bat was usually a piece of stick or a thin board. But with a child's imagination we were for the afternoon – or until the ball unraveled beyond repair – in the bottom of the ninth with bases loaded and one out to go.

We were adventurous kids and often walked down the railroad spur line. The overgrown area of bushes and vegetation behind the old chair factory was where we picked wild cherries, blackberries, and locusts. We did some dangerous things like crawling through and eighteen-inch culvert under the railroad spur that ran along Holtzclaw Avenue. This was very dangerous because getting trapped was a real possibility.

Eugene and Jeff had two aunts living across town in the Westside projects. To get there we often walked several miles from Bushtown down the railroad tracks where they intersected with Main Street. Though it was quite a distance, no one seemed to mind.

On Sunday, we sometimes walked to my grandparents' house on East Eighth Street, hoping that my Grandma might give me a nickel to buy some sherbet from Kay's Ice Cream store. We shared and shared alike small treats and confections that never amounted to much more than a bite or spoonful or two… Because that's what friends do.

Early on, none of us were allowed to go to Lincoln Park (the city's colored park) alone. But we would go there on Sunday with our parents to watch the ball games. If Mother or Pappa Will had a little extra change, Sister and I were treated to a bag of popcorn or peanuts.

This might sound strange, but my friends and I really enjoyed Sunday school. Mrs. Sena Horne, our Sunday School teacher, took a real interest in us. All of the Sunday School teachers of Orchard Knob Missionary Baptist Church – the church I would be a member of for the rest of my life – encouraged us. If we did well in school, they would give us complimentary "knothole gang" tickets so that we could go see the Chattanooga Lookouts baseball games.

Activities slowed in the winter, and we stayed closer to home. We flew kites made of sticks and the paper from dry cleaner bags. We built tent houses from anything and everything we could get our hands on. We got so good at building makeshift tent houses that once we constructed a two-story house and put a heater in it to keep us cozy and warm.

Mid-South winters for the most part were mild enough to allow us to play outside for long periods of time without getting too chilled. However, when Mother asked me to go to the store, somehow the weather would become freezing. As clever as I thought I was in trying to get out of my responsibility, Mother gave me "the look" that let me know I could never get away with stuff like that.

The kids in our group weren't the fighting kind. Other than Jeff, always trying to get even with his older brother Eugene by throwing rocks at him, we all were for the most part pretty even-tempered. In the battle of the brothers, Eugene always dodged Jeff's attacks so there was no real harm or foul although the constant failure to get revenge infuriated Jeff to no end.

Some of us became Boy Scouts. I remember riding the east Chattanooga streetcar to the end of the line to go to Hawkins Farm on Highway 58. As we traveled through what was called KKK country, we held our breath and hoped that the local white boys were not around. We knew that if they were, to protect ourselves, the most prudent thing was to run away. We all had heard there were stories about Negroes who were careless in East Chattanooga and never heard from again. And we weren't taking any chances. When we finally made it to the farm in one piece, we forgot about the white boys, swam in the pond and camped out in that safe space while all the while being surrounded by those who didn't appreciate us being in the vicinity.

In Bushtown, times were mostly good as we grew and started paying attention to the opposite sex. It wasn't unheard of for long-time playmates to one day "grow sweet" on one another – suddenly becoming girlfriends and boyfriends.

I was very shy in my early teens, as most of the kids in our little gang. I was in about the sixth grade when I told the girl next door that I liked Doris McClesky. As luck would have it, the cat would soon be out of the bag when Doris visited my neighbor later that day. She and her friends teased me to the point I went into the house and hid under the bed. But the shyness only lasted a couple more years before the fellas and I were old enough to venture out to Lincoln Park without our parents - eager to see what girls might be there on Sunday.

On one particular Sunday we ventured to Lincoln Park. On our way home, a group of boys from Fortwood surprised us on East Third Street. They demanded we stop. Usually, we would just call their bluff, shout out a couple of insults and go on about our business. But this time we were stopped cold. We obeyed their command because one of them carried a pistol.

Because they felt they had the upper hand – which they did – the Fortwood boys made us sit at the base of Engel Stadium's outfield fence. One by one they pointed us out and demanded, "Hit the viaduct!". This meant for us to run along the top of the railroad bridge over Third Street. They demanded we run its length without stopping and you best believe that's what we did. None of us were hurt, but it did shake us up knowing that a gun was in the picture, even though we were never directly threatened with it.

Times were changing. . . Or maybe time remained the same and we were the ones who were doing the changing. As we grew older and ventured out of Bushtown to a different neighborhood or another part of town meant that you had to be more aware and be prepared to protect yourself. That was especially true on the Southside of Chattanooga, where I and my classmate Benton Stovall would double date with Hilda Rakestraw and Carolyn Stone.

In those days, if you were a stranger entering to some neighborhoods, even if all the neighbors were colored, you risk being literally run out. When we were ready to go home, we would always look to see if the coast was clear before we ventured from the porch and caught the bus for the ride home.

As I grew older and thought myself to be more sophisticated, we took our dates on the Missionary Ridge streetcar route. A twenty-cent ride that took about two hours to complete. At the end of the line, the conductor always took his time to have a cigarette or two. This allowed young couples time to really enjoy the beautiful evening together.

At other times we would take our dates to the end of the Saint Elmo bus line and hike up the side of Lookout Mountain. On one occasion, my date and I went to Point Park and forgot the time. The park had closed and the gates were locked. So we had to scale the 10 foot wall to get out. Excursion trains would come from distant points to the city and we made it our and we made it our business to go down to Union Station to see what new girls had come to town.

Back in those days, while some might have considered me somewhat popular in matters of social interaction, that was only one side of my upbringing. Of those who contributed to the more intellectual and seriousness of my being, I laud my elementary, junior and Senior High School teachers who gave us not only knowledge but also a sense of self-respect.

They challenged us to dream. They inspired us to become more than a Jim Crow society could ever expect. Miss Rose McGee, my civics teacher, taught us about the history accomplishments of our people when we weren't mentioned at all in the school board issued history books. She taught us about our rights as citizens and challenged us to take a stand in whatever we did. She introduced us to the NAACP Youth Council. It was Miss Magee's teachings that whetted our curiosity about civil rights. She, along with Principal W.J. Davenport, encouraged me to become active. In the 11th grade I became chairman of the combined Councils of the Youth NAACP.

The chance that Mother took by bringing us to Chattanooga changed the circumstances of my life. Being older than my classmates I suppose I came off as more mature. I believe this had a great bearing on my future.

I graduated the 9th grade as head of my class. When I moved on to Howard High, I began writing letters to the editor of the *Chattanooga Times* newspaper, decrying segregation and discrimination.

After graduating high school in 1943, I volunteered for the Navy with my good friend Richard Kelley. But we both backed out before being sworn in. In 1945, I was ranked 1-A by the draft board but was never called to serve. By the time of the Korean War, Vi and I had four children and I was never called to service.

Somehow or another civilian leadership on behalf of my people seemed to be my future, my "calling". The choices, the "chances" we do or don't take seem to play directly into the circumstances that we find ourselves in. Together they create the road map of our lives, but that map has few straightaways and an abundant number of turns and detours. Which road to choose is as important as which road not to choose. In the 1940s, chance or circumstance was only beginning with me and for whatever the path fate had in store. . . I was on my way.

CHAPTER 5

Howard High School: An Intergenerational Connector for Change

IN 1865, AT THE BEGINNING OF the post-Civil War reconstruction error, Howard High School, my alma mater, became Chattanooga's first publicly funded school. Originally called the Howard Free School, it was named for Union General Oliver Otis Howard, head of the recently created Federal Freedmen's Bureau, which was tasked with finding ways to integrate the newly freed Negroes into a very defeated, bitter, and reluctant Southern society.

In the early years, the Howard school was located on East 11th St. The school originally consisted of grades one through 12. But as the colored population of Chattanooga grew rapidly, younger students were sent to newly established colored, elementary and junior high schools. After several moves throughout the decades in 1954, Howard High School's final destination became the 2500 block of South Market Street. In its almost 150-year history, the contributions of Howard High's alumni have not only impacted the entire city of Chattanooga, but its influence has been felt throughout the nation in the world of politics, business, education and entertainment.

Howard High's early success is the equivalent of making a silk purse out of a sow's ear. The dedicated principals and teachers with their single-minded devotion to uplift the race is a testament to the generations of black folk in America – with few resources – who perfected the art of making do.

Up until the 1960s, the colored schools of Chattanooga were the stepchildren of public education. New textbooks went to white schools, while the colored schools had to rely on outdated and vandalized books, there were often incomplete missing covers and pages.

Before the 1950s push toward desegregating the schools, Negro teachers in the public school system held more degrees per capita than their white counterparts. But they received less pay, suffered a chronic lack of teaching supplies, and had to endure overt racism emanating from the school board administration offices on down. Still, despite the odds, Howard High School managed to churn out class after class of rounded, well-educated students.

I served as the President of the 1947 class of Howard Hi. It was a class that started out with 138 tenth graders that graduated 118. Among my peers would be the first two Negro surgeons in Chattanooga, a president of a historic black university, a local school principal, and several educators.

While at Howard High, Principal W.J. Davenport and other teachers supported and encouraged me as I wrote letters to the editor decrying segregation and racial discrimination. As class president and valedictorian of the class of 47, I believe I our fulfilled Howard's practice of exceeding white expectations of what black people in our society should or could be. And thanks to that tradition of passing expectations forward my years at Howard High contributed greatly to not only shaping my future outlook and voice, but also that of my children and grandchildren.

The baton of social responsibility was successfully passed from my generation to that very special class, the Howard High School class of 1960, who took it upon themselves to topple old Jim Crow from his pedestal for all time.

On their way to the sit-in demonstrations each Howard high student carried with them a small piece of paper with eight rules for a peaceful demonstration. Be on your best behavior. No weapons.

Try to make small purchases. No profanity. Allow space in between. No loud talking. No standing in aisles. Meet at 9th and Market streets at 4:00 PM sharp.

We, as black folks, are certainly accustomed to crafting miracles from the simplest of things. When it came to Howard High school students in their quest for social justice… this simple list would prove to be the recipe for success.

James Mapp and Sit-In Students From 1960 Honored at Baylor School in 2010

Seated - James Mapp, Virgil Roberson, JoAnne Favors and Paul Walker
Standing - Robert Parks, Billy Edwards, Leaman Pierce and Dr. William Taylor

CHAPTER 6

Professional Life

WORKING YEARS

IN 1939 AT THE AGE OF 12, I went to work for Clonts grocery store on Cleveland Avenue. When Clonts closed a few months later, I then found a job with Sol Kopkins grocery next door where I worked during the school year from 1939 to 1945. In the summers of '44 to '47 – the final years of World War Two – I was employed at US Steel and foundry, supplying equipment to the U.S. military.

Rail thin and weighing about 135 pounds soaking wet, I and most other Colored workers were designated as utility men – routinely assigned the nastier tasks at the foundry. One of our main jobs was unloading from open railroad cars the processed coal called coke. Especially during the summer, it was one of the hottest jobs at the plant. Inside the huge building was no better as the blast furnaces radiated heat everywhere. We mostly survived the 10-hour work shift on salt tablets and water.

During the foundry days, I tried my best to eat everything in sight. In the morning I consumed eight to ten biscuits plus meat, eggs, and grits. At the foundry – lucky for us – lunch was a heavy, filling meal. The negro cooks could really turn it out. But after shifts lasting ten long hours every bit of fuel I consumed was gone. After dinner at home, I ate every leftover in sight. I was an eating machine.

In the evening I would go down to East Ninth Street to buy milk shakes and sundries. But no matter what I did and how much I ate, I still weighed no more than 135 pounds.

At the foundry I did almost every dangerous, dirty job imaginable. But my mother's eldest brother, the Reverend Uncle Willie Hargrove, refused to allow me to pour iron. That was just too dangerous. Uncle Willie had been around a long time and he knew what he was talking about.

At the foundry Uncle Willie was a distinct and different kind of Colored man. He was a bit of a ladies' man and always presented himself in "just so" fashion. How he presented himself even extended to his work. Uncle Willie was a core maker who wore white shirts and white overalls to work. All other core makers who used the black sand for making castings got downright filthy, but Uncle Willie managed to stay pretty much unsoiled as he deliberately went about his work. Even then he regularly produced more cores than anyone else on the floor.

At the foundry it was a long held understanding that race was a determining factor in how much you were to be paid. I remember when the AFL (American Federation of Labor) sent union representatives for contract renewals between the local workers and plant management. Negroes were making 50 cents per hour while white workers were making up to 75 cents.

But interestingly enough, the discrimination didn't end there. It was common knowledge that among all the workers at the Chattanooga plant that both Negro and white union members in Chicago and Pittsburg made the whopping sum of $1.25 an hour. This chafed the local white workers to no end. But somehow in their figuring, the two types of pay discrimination weren't the same.

In my eyes the "southern penalty" was discrimination on top of discrimination. One would think that the Southern white workers might realize the sameness of it all and find some empathy for Negro workers. But to admit such an understanding would fly in the face of everything they held dear in a segregated society.

On one particular day the union representative brought us black workers together (we didn't mingle with the white union workers) and announced, "You boys will receive a raise of three cents an hour". But it was quickly found out that the white workers would receive a boost of ten cents an hour. Talk about adding insult to injury . . . It was obvious that the union didn't have our best interest in mind, and this was enough to stir even the most complacent of us into action. So, we voted out the AFL and voted in its competitor, the CIO (the Congress of Industrial Organizations), which worked on our behalf to raise our salaries.

During the school year I returned to work at the local stores where I was known around the neighborhood as "Buddy the grocery boy". I worked for Ben Mott and became a butcher and then manager and continued to work there until February of '49.

Being held back for two full academic years during my elementary school days meant that I was older than all my classmates. I was two months short of my twentieth birthday when I graduated from Howard High. After U.S. Steel, I took summer jobs at Milne Chair Factory and Railway Express, a parcel shipping company, where I made $56.00 every two weeks. It was from this job that I was able to save enough for college. I moved to Nashville and attended Tennessee A & I University (later renamed Tennessee State) for a few semesters. There I met Vi. We fell in love, got married and moved back to Chattanooga. In January of '49 our first child was born . . . a girl named Brenda.

Once back in Chattanooga, I started a new career working for the North Carolina Mutual Insurance Company. I was what is know as a "debit" insurance agent. This meant my job was to go door to door collecting insurance premiums on our customers policies.

One day as I walked down Greenwood Avenue, Mr. Wiley – a much older gentleman – called me aside. He advised me that I needed to get rid of the insurance collection book. In his words, "Get a loaf of bread", instead. I knew what he meant. He didn't think I was being practical in my pursuit and that I should have a more traditional job - more typical of a Colored man with a family.

At that time, I was regarded as a new king of "negro" that many who considered themselves "regular folk" didn't understand. Any job that was seen as "white collar" was looked upon with suspicion. Many thought poorly of black people venturing out of their traditional blue and brown collar stations. But with a new wife and new child at home, and a burning desire to be more that what was expected of me . . . To Mr. Wiley, I smiled and kept collecting my debit. I worked as a debit collector two years until one Wednesday, after finishing my report, I suddenly decided to quit in order to return to Nashville to Tennessee A&I in the hope of getting my wife and me back into college.

I quit the insurance job on a Wednesday, went to Nashville on a Thursday, and got a job with McKissack Construction (the oldest Black construction company in America) that Friday. At the time laborers were making $0.75 per hour. I did construction work and sent home everything I made except $8.00 per week. By then our second child, Deborah, was born and a third was only a month away. While I was determined to return to school and did all I could, unfortunately time and circumstance told me it wasn't in the cards.

So, I returned to Chattanooga to work for North Carolina Mutual again. Within the year I was promoted to staff manager. I remained in that position until 1964 when I was demoted back to the position of debit collector. Upper management claimed that although I did my job and did it well, the demotion was due to what they considered an excessive amount of time I had spent in court on the school system desegregation case. Fortunately for me, Union Protective Insurance Company needed a district manager. So instead of being demoted, the new opportunity provided me a leg up in my career.

My stay with Union Protective would last only one year. I was one of the highest paid managers in the system. But because of what turned out to be a moral conflict, that good thing would come to a sudden end. As I remember, a young man with a $500 policy was killed. I sent in the paperwork to get his beneficiary's money but instead I was instructed to take $250 in small bills to settle the claim with his family. I wrote back saying, "I am of the opinion that the claim should be paid or rejected". The $500 check was sent. Shortly thereafter a managers' meeting was held at the home office and I was singled out as one who wouldn't play ball by compromising claims. After this meeting the agency director and I mutually agreed that we should part company.

I was brought up to believe that "fair is fair" and there were just some principles that a man of faith must refuse to sacrifice.

LIFE AS AN ENTREPRENEUR

In the spring of '65, not long after parting ways with Union Protective, Vi and I tossed around the idea of opening my own insurance agency. Soon after, the James R. Mapp General Insurance Agency was born. This independent move wasn't by any means a walk in the park. Rather it marked the beginning of a hardship year. Between April of 1965 to April of 1966, my earnings were a mere $1,600 to support a family with eight children. By then our youngest was now of school age and this allowed Vi to supplement our income by working as a teacher's aide at Sunnyside Elementary for $800 per year. No question, we were in the financial struggles of our lives.

Being the president of the local branch of the NAACP, people had a few assumptions, especially when it came to our income status or assumed wealth. You'd be surprised how folks would correlate my being in the local newspapers and on television with how much money people thought we had.

No duties that I or other officials performed on behalf of the NAACP put money in our pockets. With the exception of drastically modified fees for lawyers and legal expenses, almost everything that was done on behalf of desegregating the schools in Chattanooga was accomplished on a voluntary basis. We all sacrificed our time, our effort, and our personal safety for our mutual benefit. To give without reservation is the price we paid to achieve equality and freedom. The Mapp family was as poor as Job's turkey but remained rich in hope and determination.

As a newly independent businessman, I sold my first fire policy on a building across the street from where I set up my office at 9th and

University streets. It was a proud moment. The premium was $208 and my commission was $52.00. After leaving Union Protective I was drawing unemployment compensation. I was so impressed with myself that I made the mistake of bragging to the unemployment officer about the commission I had just earned. As a result of my new income, they cut off my compensation.

And if things couldn't have gotten worse, the fire and casualty company holding the new policy told me that I could not insure restaurants. The way I looked at it I was insuring the building, not the restaurant. They canceled the policy anyway, and I had to return my first commission. I was conducting my new business from the NAACP office because I had yet to receive all of my required licenses. My landlord, Carver Investment Company, stated that since I was now running a "business" I had to start paying rent separately or they were going to increase the NAACP's rent as compensation. I couldn't have that, so I started paying rent. On the upside, this gave me the chance to move my office from the middle room to the front of the building to witness at street level the day's events. And I was proud to stand behind the plate glass window that read James R. Mapp General Insurance Agency.

Through it all, I am proud to say that the Mapp family made it through. We weathered the storms, learned a lot of life lessons, and although the new business was constantly on the edge...we never declared bankruptcy.

At the time, Richard Smith (owner of the Sinclair Agency) and I were both seeking independent casualty insurance agency contracts. We visited Nashville several times in an effort to get the commissioner of insurance to open the door for us, but to no avail. The big independent agencies were moving to get rid of us smaller fry. This included white agencies as well. We discovered that there were only two blacks in the state with independent general agency contracts. One was held by a black bank in Nashville that had a contract (since 1906), and the other was by a black man who had become a partner with a Jewish businessman. The Jewish man died and the black partner was allowed to retain the business through the previous association.

In 1967 I applied for a small-business loan, only to be turned down because of race. At that time, no black person in Tennessee had been able to get a small-business loan. It would be years before blacks could participate and be accepted on their own merits.

1969 was a busy year for me. I maintained my insurance business on a part-time basis as I went to work full time for the newly established federally funded Model Cities Program, an element of Lyndon Johnson's Great Society and war on poverty. I had kept my insurance agency open by marketing nonstandard fire and auto insurance. In '69 I also passed the test and got my real estate license. This gave me an added outlet to earn a living. A few years later, I became a real estate broker.

Although I worked fifty-plus hours a week, I still spent countless hours dealing with others' problems through the NAACP. One would think that this would be a boon to my business by way of new clients, but most folks never even thought to reciprocate in kind by bringing or referring insurance business my way. It's as if they were dealing with two separate people. Folks came to the NAACP office that was adjacent to mine past the painted sign on the plate glass window that told of my General Insurance Agency. But somehow or another the connection was rarely made.

Another way my business suffered was because of Blacks who were up the ladder in influential positions. They could have lent real financial support by referring business my way, but mostly avoided association with me due to their own political and business reasons.

I'm telling you…it's tough to fight battles for others with such little support. In many ways I suppose I became an island unto myself because I insisted on forging ahead with the notion that "change is good and in the end we all will be better for it". Don't get me wrong…Simple heartfelt thanks were most certainly appreciated and cherished, but when it came to providing food and a roof over me and my family…" thanks" did little to "feed the kitty".

Blacks with lesser incomes were primary customers. I was

occasionally surprised when even knowing about my history and affiliation with the NAACP, a few from the white community patronized my insurance business as well. When they felt they had been wronged by their own, they'd seek me out as an alternative. And a few actually brought other white customers to my company.

I will always remember one of my white clients from East Brainerd who was dissatisfied with an insurance agency which he had been doing business with for years. He came into my office wearing overalls. I took time to talk with him about his insurance, and he appreciated the fact that I was not put off by his appearance. We had a long conversation. He brought in his homeowners insurance policy, and when it came time to pay, he reached into the bib of his overalls and pulled out a wad of bills to pay the entire premium for the year. The man thanked me for taking the time to hear his questions and supply answers. He later brought his rental properties for me to insure as well. He then referred his son-in-law, and they continued to purchase insurance from me until my parent company canceled all insurance coverage in Tennessee and pulled out of the state.

MODEL CITIES YEARS

In 1969 I went to work for the Model Cities Program, a federal urban renewal government program. Our objective was supposed to be urban renewal for lower income areas. Because I was president of the NAACP, I was the only entry-level employee of the program who had to have approval of the entire city commission to be hired.

My first assignment was to develop a system for gathering data on what was called the "model neighborhood". I set up a system that met the needs of the program. I was advanced to the position of housing planner. I had recently received my license as an affiliate broker with Carver Investment Company, so this was a natural for me. During the week I would leave Model Cities at four in the afternoon, go to my insurance / real estate office, and stay until six or six thirty in the evening. I also took my Model Cities lunch hour at my office which was also open on Saturdays.

With Model Cities I had a volunteer task force with great latitude in setting the agenda. Our role was to come up with plans that would change the decaying urban area and make it a model, up-to-date, livable community. But then Congress passed the Green Amendment in the early '70s, and community input was diluted and the power of change was shifted to the Mayor's office.

Our task force had the support of the Department of Housing and Urban Development (HUD), which had mandated an open housing ordinance to be included in the housing program and did not restrict where Blacks can live. Mayor Robert Kirk Walker's office wanted it to only cover the model neighborhood, but HUD demanded that this ordinance cover the entire city. The mayor's office fought to stop the city-wide implementation.

At Model Cities, we developed a nonprofit housing corporation that was very comprehensive and included a minority builders' support system, a revolving loan fund, a land banking area, so that builders could compete in the housing market. An outsider from Boston was hired to administer the program, despite the fact that I had developed it.

The housing corporation was so promising that it was chartered with the state and approved for funding in Washington. Our legal counsel was Benny J. Harris, who would later become the first black city judge. We had set up our corporate staff and were ready to do business. Mayor Walker objected, but he could not stop it. In 1972 the funds were allocated for us to go to work but soon after, President Nixon announced a moratorium on housing which killed most of the components of the program.

The city tried every way imaginable to circumvent the enactment of the open housing ordinance. But we had successfully reached out and recruited ministers from both races for their support. Between this alliance, the support of the NAACP, and others, the city officials could not overcome such a sizable coalition. This alliance helped me keep my job while actively bucking our city bosses' wishes. The payback for coalition building has its merits, indeed!

As we worked on the open housing ordinance, the director of

45

the Model Cities Program ordered me to stop talking with members of the task force. I obeyed but then I had the chairman of the task force invite the director to a meeting. He came. I stood before the task force and said that this director had ordered me not to talk to them about the open housing ordinance. Caught, he turned red as a beet, apologized to the task force and openly gave me permission to pursue passage of the ordinance. The ordinance was eventually passed despite the mayor's objection.

As president of the local NAACP branch, I brought a suit against the city on behalf of Model Cities. The suit was *Dupree v. the City of Chattanooga*. I continued the school desegregation suit, *Mapp v. the Chattanooga Board of Education*. All the while I was still employed by Model Cities. In April 1971 I spent almost all working days in federal court. While many city employees, including Model Cities employees, were in the courtroom testifying they were all on payroll. I was the only one not on payroll. Fortunately, I had accumulated a lot of compensatory time, which covered my loss.

When it came time for my evaluation for Model Cities, I was given a poor rating in every area although I had never been late and had no unexcused absences. The evaluation stated that I showed no initiative, even though I had planned the data-gathering system, had my major project approved for funding in Washington and was involved in the passage of the open housing ordinance. The only way to get rid of me was to wipe out the whole planning department and transfer those duties to another agency. They did that by combining the Model Cities Program with the Community Action Program.

Mr. Harry McKeldin, who assumed head of both Model Cities and the Community Action Program, called me into his office to make me an offer that came from City Hall. He said that if I would quiet down on racial matters, he could find another job with the city for me. I saw this as selling out and immediately told him no. He respected me for my decision and later told me this was a task he did not relish.

The sad commentary of all this was that no member of either the Model Cities board or the task force spoke up when the program was being cut. After the planning department had been closed, some board members seeking advice sought me out as president of the NAACP. While employed, they didn't contend the closure of their division. But only after the cow was gone because the barn door had been closed too late, did they seek to protect their jobs.

In 1973 when the planning division closed down, I left Model Cities. I worked full-time at my insurance and real estate business. I struggled as my income dropped from more than $15,000 to $3,500 for the first two years after leaving the program. Having been through tough times before, Vi continued to work as an aide in the school system.

Because of my stance in issues that impacted others, it seemed that adequate income eluded the Mapp family for much of my adult life. Vi and I knew the risks. We knew the consequences. And we also knew that it was our mission on this earth to leave as much of a positive impact so our children and their children could prosper.

We became familiar with all of the tricks that helped get us by when times were lean. I remember saving small packages of peanut butter crackers to eat just before a meeting so that my stomach would not growl. With Vi and my eight children by my side...the lean times were still good times.

CHAPTER 7
Politics and Community

I FIRST REGISTERED TO VOTE AT THE age of twenty-one. In sixty-six years I have only missed three elections. This was because I wasn't able to get to the poll in time because of work.

By the late 1950s the Twelfth Ward, Fourth Precinct Civic League (the 12-4) was organized in Bushtown, Churchville and Orchard Knob areas to give political strength to those communities. In the 12-4 Civic League blacks instead of whites were the prominent donors. Harry Cooke, Walter Johnson and James (Fats) McClellan independently financed activities. No candidate contributions were allowed. My pastor, the Reverend William A. Dennis of the Orchard Knob Missionary Baptist Church was chairman of the League. Percy Billingsley was precinct chairman, and I was the secretary.

The Orchard Knob Missionary Baptist Church was located in the center of the 12-4's territory. Its membership figured prominently in the politics of the community. We were independent and could ask – or maybe I should say demand – policies that were good for our precinct.

When Mr. James "Bookie" Turner ran for sheriff of Hamilton County, he came to the league seeking support. The Civic League told him we did not want his money, but should he win the election we did want him to appoint a black process server. He agreed and the 12-4 backed his candidacy. Bookie Turner won, and he kept his promise by hiring Samuel Wilkins as the first black process server since 1911.

In 1962, I was part of the Chattanooga delegation that met in Nashville at Fisk University to form the Tennessee Voters Council, an organization with Black representatives from across the state. Our goal was to set into motion policies that would carry weight politically across the state and in local politics.

My entry in local politics as a candidate began in 1966. A white candidate for the county council had been given the opportunity to make a speech in the basement of Orchard Knob Missionary Baptist Church where I was a member. Immediately after he finished his speech, I decided right then and there to announce that I intended to run for the county council as well. I completed my qualifying papers and gathered the proper number of signatures. With blacks constituting less than 30 percent of the county population, I lost. But on the upside, no black had run for such a position since 1911 and I believe that election signaled a positive change in the attitudes of blacks of our county.

With experience now under my belt, in 1968 I qualified and ran for the office of county trustee. I did not seek permission from the established black political leadership and my candidacy angered those who had already committed themselves to Bill Noble, a well-known white candidate. I had very little financing and only a small group of supporters, while my opponent was financially well heeled. As dirty tricks are part of the political game, it was during this election that questions arose regarding my handling of NAACP funds. There were also questions raised about whether I could get bonded for the trustee position which required handling county funds.

Mr. C.B. Robinson, one of my fellow church members and an NAACP executive committee member, publicly questioned my ability to get bonded even though I had been continuously bonded for almost twenty years. Secondly, he questioned my handling of NAACP finances. It was at the time I was about to lose my home and needed $265, which the executive committee voted to lend me.

I had already paid some of the money back when the committee moved to forgive the balance.

Without anger or animosity and to refute the appearance of division among the Negro community, I wrote a letter to the *Chattanooga Times* praising the contributions to the community and city that Mr. Robinson had made. Although the questions he raised were without foundation, it's an example the lengths to which some will go to prevent one from being elected. I lost the election, but the next time I ran for office, Mr. C.B. Robinson worked at the voting polls on my behalf.

Although I lost the race, it brought about a keener awareness on the part of my people to participate in the local political process. Other blacks in Hamilton County began to seek political office. Lawrence Curry and the Reverend Robert Richards ran for constable, and both won. It is important to note that Lawrence Curry later threatened to arrest then Sheriff Bookie Turner, who was white, and soon afterwards the constable positions were eliminated. It's obvious that they represented too much power for a black man to have in the county.

I ran for office again in 1974 for the county register of deeds against Mrs. Shelby Brammer, an eighteen-year incumbent. Here again I lost the race, but I beat her so handily in the inner city – Mr. C.B. Robinson decided to retire as school principal and run for the Twenty-Eighth Legislative District. This was the only time that I had received a sizable contribution of votes from the white community. It also helped that Commissioner John P. Franklin carried me on the ticket with Jake Butcher, who was running for governor. Other than this help, I had received less than $400 from the white community in three prior races that I had run. In my last race, Commissioner Franklin was instrumental in giving me support in the amount of $2,000.

In that election, Mr. Robinson won the state legislative seat and served with distinction for some eighteen years. The legislative seat gained has been under black control ever since. At the state capital, Mr. Robinson joined with the state senator from Nashville,

Attorney Avon Williams, to organize the Tennessee Black Caucus. This represented a great advance for Black people statewide.

Upon Mr. Robinson's retirement from the legislature, Dr. Tommie F. Brown was elected and served many years. Always keeping her people in mind, she gained a great amount of respect in the House of Representatives and offered bills that greatly benefited the community. We have since elected another black to the legislature, Mrs. JoAnne Favors.

In 1978 I ran for the county council again and qualified. However, there was a change in the form of county government. It went from a council for to a commission form, which brought about elections by district. I had kept the door open by qualifying as the only black but with the change in districts I had to qualify again, and this time Reverend Paul A. McDaniel decided to qualify also. He was pastor of Second Missionary Baptist Church with a sizable congregation. He won and served some eighteen years.

During the 1990s there was a move to get more representation in city government. Initially four of the nine members of the new council were black. In 1990 there was a court challenge to at-large voting. The court ruled that for equitable representation candidates must run from individual districts rather than at large. It is worth noting that the change in the form of government took Chattanooga back to a time after the Civil War when Negroes numbered around 42 percent of the population of the city and were well represented as aldermen until the Legislative Act of 1911 shut Negro elected officials out by implementing at-large voting. As it turns out, when it comes to proper political representation, Chattanooga's government was right the first time.

CHAPTER 8

Involvement In The Church

I HAVE BEEN A MEMBER OF ORCHARD Knob Missionary Baptist Church for my entire adult life. In the 125 plus years since it was organized, there has never been a split in the congregation, and it has never moved more than a block from its first building. However, Highland Park Baptist Church, an all-white congregation, had originally been named Orchard Knob Baptist Church. In 1890 they sought to regain the Orchard Knob name. However, Orchard Knob Missionary Baptist Church challenged Highland Park Baptist Church for its very name and won. A great deal of progressive leadership continues to come from Orchard Knob Missionary Baptist Church to this day.

Since my advent into politics started at the Orchard Knob Missionary Baptist Church, it seems appropriate that I discuss my history with it. I started attending Orchard Knob in 1937 when I first came to Chattanooga; however, it would be five years before I became a member. I have served in many positions in the church, starting in Sunday School. I got started early in service to my church by becoming a member of the Junior Usher Board and somehow was placed in leadership positions in the mid 1940s.

As a youth I attended the Baptist Training Union and would later serve as its director. I became a member of the senior choir in my twenties and served for more than fifty-five years. I served as president of the choir for a number of years and also served as a member of the male chorus. I was a Sunday school teacher and also superintendent of the Sunday school for a number of years.

In 1962 I became the youngest trustee at Orchard Knob. Ten years later I became its chairman. It was under my and Reverend Harold K. Lester's leadership that our new church and education building were built in 1977. Reverend Lester, the longest tenured pastor of Orchard Knob, served the church for forty-six years. Through our efforts the church's twenty-year mortgage was paid off in ten years.

Here and again chance and circumstance would come into play. As it so happened, I was serving on the Model Cities staff at the time of rebuilding the church. This put me in a position to have information about the ongoing Urban Renewal Program. Because of my involvement, the church was able to get paid for our condemned church building, retain the land, and receive $38,000 from urban renewal funds.

In 1994, I was an initial member of the Orchard Knob Housing Development Board that was permitted to build forty-four apartment units. Our board was one of the first black groups in Tennessee to obtain this kind of grant. True to form, I had to push hard to get black companies included within the scope of the project. Getting the housing allocation was not easy. I selected the Otey Property Management Company out of Nashville (a Negro contractor) to manage the project.

HUD required that Orchard Knob become a partner with Chattanooga Neighborhood Enterprise (CNE) to complete the project even though the CNE had no multifamily experience and no financial interest. Here we felt that race was a factor as the city administrators didn't trust us in the decision-making process.

I knew that in order to give protection to the trustees on the Board, we needed to be incorporated. This move troubled many of the deacons of the church who felt that power had been taken away, In the end, a compromise was reached and some deacons, the pastor and a few lay members became part of the corporate body.

Prior to the building of the new church and apartments, in the 1970s I fought the Chattanooga Housing Authority and HUD's

Urban Renewal program and I was successful in getting them to reverse their decision to build on small, concentrated lots in areas across from our church property. Such small lots were usually precursors to crowded housing that would eventually become slums. I did this without the support of the church or the board of trustees. In response, the board wrote a letter to HUD distancing themselves from my actions. But in the end, faith won out over fear as larger lot sizes were developed to accommodate family-style housing.

The Orchard Knob Church played a pivotal role in scouting and yielded some of the first black Eagle Scouts. I became active in scouting in 1942 and served for more than fifty years in some capacity. In '46 I became an Eagle Scout and served as Cub and Scout Master. I was also on the board of directors of the Cherokee Area Council. Thirty years earlier we had to fight to become a segregated division of that council. At Orchard Knob I set up an umbrella group for scouting where the Explorer Scouts, Boy Scouts, Girl Scouts, and Cub Scouts were budgetary items in the church budget annually.

Membership at Orchard Knob provided me the opportunity to meet such people as Mr. James L. Jenkins, a school principal and later a member of the Chattanooga School Board od Education. Mr. Jenkins was the first black paid scout executive in the United States and became head of the segregated Dynamo Division of the Cherokee Area Council. But unlike the chairmen of white division, Mr. Jenkins had no vote or voice on the Scout's board. Dr. Lonnie Boaz and I were part of the group that challenged the racial separation. As a result of our challenge, instead of integrating the Dynamo Division, it was disbanded. This was a direct slap in the face of blacks in Scouting.

Mr. John H. Jenkins (brother of Mr. James Jenkins) was also an avid scouter, as was their father. He was Scout Master of Troop 97 for many years and was a railroad employee who gave his time and money to the program. John Jenkins was also one of the early makers of construction building blocks and built a cabin for our troop to meet near the Third Street viaduct in the early 1950s. We were modern in that we had a generator to furnish lighting, and the boys really had fun. It was here that some of the great men of our time were nurtured.

Dr. Roland Carter, an internationally renowned composer, was a boy scout in Troop 97. Others included Chief Ralph Cothran, who became the first black police chief in Chattanooga; Deputy Chief Richard Thurman, who became the highest-ranking black officer in the Hamilton County Sheriff's office; and Kenneth Owen, an architect who now lives in Birmingham, Alabama. I mention all this to show the kind of leaders that were produced in Troop 97 and to show my pride in having played a role in their lives. Chief Ralph Cothran was discussing leaders who influenced him and many other lives in the Bushtown community. Then he abruptly stopped and said to me, "You were our example and our role model". This statement delighted my heart.

Key Programs, Values Keep Scouts on Track
James Mapp shows his Eagle Scout card that bears the signature of President Harry S. Truman. He earned the honor in 1947 and later was a Scoutmaster. "Right from the beginning Scouting kept me on the right track," Mr. Mapp said. "Scouting is very much needed for growth and development of young men," he said [photo caption]. *Chattanooga Times* • *Chattanooga Free Press* archives, February 28, 2000.

Mr. John Jenkins played another role in my life as a teen. He taught me how to drive and took me to get my driver's license. I will never forget that while I was learning how to drive, I almost ran into Chickamauga Lake because I did not cut sharply enough. He took it very calmly and still continued to give me lessons. I can say that any achievement that I had in scouting was the result of his interest in me.

Although early on we had our differences, I had a chance to meet and get to know Mr. C.B. Robinson as a neighbor and a fellow church member. We developed a respect for each other. He was a school principal and was nationally known in labor circles and later became a Tennessee state representative, where he gave some eighteen years of outstanding service. He was the last principal to drop the Youth Council of the NAACP from his program at the insistence of the school superintendent and school board. I had the privilege of bringing Mr. Robinson to the board of trustees of Orchard Knob Missionary Baptist Church, where he had been shunned by the board for many ears. He later became the chairman of the corporate board, and his influence was a deciding factor in financing our new church.

Throughout these many decades my membership with Orchard Knob Missionary Baptist church has taught me how to be a leader and a mindful servant who strives to keep ethics, decency and fair play at the center of my life.

CHAPTER 9

NAACP Years (National Association for the Advancement of Colored People)

MY ASSOCIATION WITH THE NAACP BEGAN at Orchard Knob Junior High school in 1942. At that time all Negro schools had NAACP youth councils. Dues were ten cents a year. In high school I was elected president and in 1946 became chairman of youth councils citywide.

EARLY INSPIRATION

One of the most inspiring people who convinced me of the value of being active and uncompromising when it came to the demands of the NAACP was Mrs. Ruby Hurley, who I first met in 1945. Mrs. Hurley had been sent to Chattanooga by Walter White, the executive secretary of the national NAACP. Her mission was to organize the youth of the Southeast. With Mrs. Hurley I attended the first Southeast Region Youth Conference at Dillard University in New Orleans in 1946.

Mrs. Hurley did such a good job of recruiting youth in the southeast region that she was elevated to organize the adults as well. She was so successful in Birmingham that in 1956 the state legislature of Alabama actually voted to outlaw the NAACP. After that, Mrs.

Hurley was forced to move her office to Atlanta, but in Alabama the NAACP she helped build continued to function underground.

Ruby Hurley's influence was so prominent in Alabama's NAACP that I sometimes wondered how much effect it had in contributing to the legacy of Dr. King . . . and especially the Montgomery bus boycott. Not to take anything away from Dr. King's achievements, it is important to acknowledge the contributions of those in the trenches who helped build and support those in the forefront.

Mrs. Hurley was actively targeted by hate groups who sought to harm or kill her. But there were good white friends who protected her as she slipped in and out of southern cities. One such friend was Mr. John H. Popham, a reporter for the *New York Times* and later the editor of the *Chattanooga Times*. Mr. Popham often told of occasions when Mrs. Hurley had to be rescued from angry mobs. She was fearless in her mission and a great inspiration and force to be reckoned with.

AN ASPIRING LEADER

In 1959, uprisings among black college students were occurring across the country. White fear and anger was prevalent across the South. As these elements added up to potential danger, leaders to spearhead positions of the NAACP were hard to find. And this was the case in Chattanooga.

I was first elected as the Chattanooga branch secretary in 1953 and served until 1959. As secretary I served under several presidents, including Dr. P. A. Stephens (a medical doctor), who first chartered the branch.

In 1959, at the age of 32, I became president of the Chattanooga branch of the NAACP. However, I was not the membership's first choice. A local pastor had been elected but stepped down, leaving the way open for me to become president.

As the newly elected president, I had many questions. Many self-doubts. Would I be the head of an action-oriented leadership that would upend what I considered to be the milder past practices of the branch? Would I confuse and anger those Blacks and whites who thought that race relationships were relatively good and there was no need for change? Would there be dangerous pushback across the city from white racists? Would I be satisfied with the status quo of things or press forward for change without compromise? I suppose that many of these questions and self-doubts hinged on whether the executive committee would accept me and if the general membership would embrace me as their leader.

During my first term of office, I was a delegate at the NAACP National Convention in St. Paul, Minnesota. It was there I would realize just how ingrained in me the practice of racial separation really was. In Chattanooga it was rare for blacks and whites to socially meet in individual homes, but to mingle in public – that was another matter.

In St. Paul, things were very different. It was common practice for the races to mingle where they pleased. While at the convention, during social hours I was reluctant—or maybe I should say "scared"— when I had an opportunity to dance with a white woman. Although I was a thousand miles from the Deep South it became apparent real quick that the restrictions I had grown up with had followed me to Minnesota. The attitudes of white people there were very different from even the northern cities like Chicago and New York. Everywhere we went, Blacks were treated as valued customers.

During the St. Paul convention, I had opportunities to learn firsthand of the sacrifices made by many Negroes across the nation. Through these conversations I learned in depth about their struggle for equality. I also learned about the many programs that were initiated by the NAACP national leadership. This added to my desire to make change. Hearing the stories of fellow southerners in places much more dangerous than moderate Chattanooga motivated me.

After the day's meetings, a number of us attended the convention on shoestring budgets and would not go into the nightclubs because we barely had the money to even buy a Coke. So, we would mill around outside and talk amongst ourselves.

When I came on the scene as the new president, the Chattanooga

NAACP branch didn't even have an office or a telephone. Fortunately, there were some executive committee members who felt that the time had come to at least have a place where we could meet freely at any time. It was a small office but donated furniture, a desk, telephone and a few chairs made the space feel official.

From its inception, the Chattanooga branch has dealt with many of the problems including equalization of teachers' salaries, the school-desegregation suit, and assisting neighborhood communities in Tennessee and Georgia who were in need. We also helped establish other branches in nearby towns and assisted with discrimination problems that people encountered there.

I had grown up in the NAACP since I was a teen so as the newly elected branch president, I had some ideas of how to lead. Although I was not yet polished and lacked social standing, I had nerve enough to speak up when the occasion demanded it. To the surprise of many, I rejected what I considered patronizing efforts from the white community. I saw their overtures as a way of maintaining levels of control. It was indeed a new day, and I was the new Negro to deal with.

I made moves to change the long held racial status quo and was not shy about asking for changes – sometimes radical changes – in the way things had been previously done. I had almost no relationship with the white and black movers and shakers of Chattanooga's power set. My intention was to completely alter the centuries old social fabric of my city once and for all.

My desire for racial advancement was no secret, and there were fears in the black and white communities that my approach to issues of segregation and racial discrimination were too fast too soon. I suppose much of my independent streak was bolstered by the fact that I derived my employment from a Negro insurance firm or by my own hand.

It took a while for Chattanoogans to get used to me and my tactics. There were times that the pushback from my own Black community made me questions "did they really want true progress, or is it just lip service?" I wondered why so many would or could accept so little and call it progress.

As a result of what was considered my "militancy", I would often feel alone. I knew that some people kept their distance because they feared that any association with this outspoken man named James Mapp could cost them their community standing or even their jobs. I knew that if I pondered too hard on this or let it bother me, I couldn't fulfill my mission. That was their problem…not mine. Fortunately for company, I had Vi and our eight kids. And for them I was determined to do whatever was required. Along the way I learned that so much of success is built on a wing and especially a prayer.

In November of 1959, as president of the local chapter, I was sent to Nashville as one of the Chattanooga delegation of the NAACP state Conference of Branches. The church in which we met was next to Brown's hotel which charged only two dollars a night. We were expected to pay for our own lodging, and I didn't have enough money to get a room. So, I slept in my old station wagon behind the church with only my overcoat to cover me that cold night. The next morning the janitor came early, and I was able to go inside and freshen up so that would be no telltale signs of how I spent the night. My reward came in the first session where I learned how a school desegregation suit could be filed. When I returned to Chattanooga, I had the knowledge and was eager to put what I had learned to the test.

Left to right: Dr. Major Jones, the Reverend Dogan Williams, Dr. M.L. King Jr., Dr. Horace Traylor (Council for Cooperative Action), and James R. Mapp (president, NAACP). This Christian leadership group joined the local branch of the NAACP to celebrate the Emancipation Proclamation on January 1, 1960, at Memorial Auditorium in downtown Chattanooga. Personal Collection.

THWARTING TROUBLE

During my second term as president, the branch joined the effort in Gulfport, Mississippi. The National NAACP was being sued and the organization faced the very real threat of being put out of business if they could not post a million-dollar bond. The case involved boycotting of a store in Gulfport because of its racially discriminatory practices. The merchant suing had claimed the NAACP had damaged his business by boycotting him.

Although other groups were involved in the suit, the NAACP was singled out because of its national profile. The NAACP was in dire straits as it sought to solicit the funds required. At that time national board members thought we should accept the donations from outside supporters such as the labor unions or Jewish groups.

But others felt that these contributions might be used as leverage to modify or compromise our stand on affirmative action. If there ever was a time for national action, this was it. The very existence of the NAACP was at stake and all local chapters needed to stand tall.

In Chattanooga, we heard the call. People who earned as little as fifteen dollars per week walked into our office to donate. To accommodate those who could not come during working hours, I opened the NAACP office on Saturday and sometimes on Sunday to receive their contributions. During the week I also accepted funds at my insurance office.

Both the labor union and Jewish group proposed that we drop, modify or water-down some of our affirmative action goals. The national office didn't hesitate to say "no". In the end, the NAACP membership persevered raising the needed funds through our own resources and abilities.

Throughout this crisis, I was very heartened that Blacks in Chattanooga responded so positively to the national call for help. As president of the branch, I almost single-handedly managed the fund-raising which lasted some thirteen weeks. We collected in all over $13,000.

It was an important national victory, since the NAACP had previously been banned in neighboring Alabama. Many outsiders wanted to help, but our faith in our community and in a higher power gave us the wherewithal to achieve this great victory on our own.

I learned a great lesson regarding self-reliance when making a stand. I also learned that those who might be counted as friends or allies may support you, but when it comes to fulfilling their agenda, all bets are off.

BUSINESS AS USUAL

When complaints were alleged or filed against a business or organization and the NAACP was asked to intervene, I followed this process:

- Get all the information from the complainant.

- Gather basic data on the general practice of hiring and promotions, including the total number of employees by race and the number of blacks in management and supervisory positions. Then compare the data.
- And bring the parties together to discuss the problem as presented by the claimant to see if there could be a resolution.
- I found over the years that if the person seeking help from the NAACP had a pretty good grasp of the problem, this made our job much easier. I always tried not to threaten any legal action unless nothing else worked. I always attempted to meet or talk with the CEO or someone in top management. I would never end the conversation or meeting without seeking to get promotions, positions upgraded, or seeking additional hiring.

In 1960 executive committee members tried to limit my role as president by illegally naming a chairman. This violated the constitution and bylaws of the national NAACP. Their purpose was to modify my more radical stance in matters of race. The committee members were angry that I carried out our purpose without regard to the feelings of white elected officials and community leaders. Fortunately, the coup attempt was short lived as the National office vetoed their methods and other members stood up to support my leadership.

After my eight-year tenure as president of the local NAACP, Mr. George Key, another Howard High graduate, followed me. Mr. Key took a different attitude regarding the NAACP's role when it came to assisting those asking for support. He demanded that a complainant should first be a member of the local branch. In order to be helped, people responded to his request for membership. Looking back, I see that his approach did place some responsibility on the person, and that was good. But many had insufficient income to pay the $10 membership fee, and I recognized that too.

Too often there is a pattern that those seeking relief seldom make an effort to become a member. And there were times when some would get angry if asked to join. There is an old axiom that says that we as a people "buy what we want and beg for what we need." To many the NAACP didn't exist until they personally encountered difficulties. Until then, they were happy to benefit from those who took time, effort, and money to make their lives easier. On contacting us, they will generally say, "Such-and-such told me I should call the NAACP and get help with my problem".

I served the Chattanooga branch of the NAACP as president for 26 years total until my retirement in 1995. Although it used up a great deal of my time, it was worth it. Fortunately for me, participation in the NAACP became a family affair. Vi was always an active participant in membership and fundraising for the local branch. She also coordinated the primary fundraising ball that was held at the Read House Hotel in the 1970's and chaired the committee that annually brought in the Ebony Fashion Fair fundraiser for years. As for our children, especially the four youngest, they were active in the youth branch and we as a family traveled to many state, regional and national conferences together. All in all... the NAACP was an organization the Mapp family was proud to be a part of.

CHAPTER 10
Attacking Discrimination In Employment

HAVING SERVED SEVERAL TERMS AS NAACP president on the state and local level, my efforts to seek equal opportunities for blacks touched many areas, including employment. I called out the local post offices for their practices of hiring few blacks and for those employed, protested their lack of promotions. In the mid-1960s we got few results. But we would see measures of success when Mr. C.B. Robinson (who worked with unions at the national level) joined us. Mr. Robinson eventually became a union representative and postmaster. Through our efforts doors were opened for new hiring and upgrading of postal positions. While there were strides toward progress as late as 2014 there continues to be concerns regarding Black hiring and promotions. This shows that for progress to continue, we can never let our guard down.

In Chattanooga, there hadn't been a black person on the draft board since 1935 until in 1960 members of the local NAACP branch picketed the federal unit until we got the change demanded. Within the federal government, we were successful in alleviating many of the discriminatory practices at the Volunteer Ordnance Works, where explosives were manufactured and stored. Complaints were filed with the local branch and we promptly settled many disputes.

The second largest military cemetery in the country is here in Chattanooga, and since the civil war, blacks had not been employed there. I telephoned officials from the federal government about this racial exclusion and eventually got results. But when I visited the cemetery in 2011, I noticed few black employees and it seemed that the clock had been turned back.

In the early 1960's under my leadership of the local NAACP branch, we moved to desegregate the whites only Baroness Erlanger hospital in its public room accommodations. From 1947 until 1962 the George Washington Carver Memorial Hospital was the primary health care facility for Chattanooga's Negroes. Formerly the Old West Ellis Hospital, Carver was said to be the first municipality owned tax supported hospital in America that was staffed by Negro doctors, nurses and other personnel. Nevertheless, since city funds were involved, it was overseen by a white administrator.

While black doctors were not officially allowed to practice in Erlanger Hospital, Doctor Looney, a black physician and one of the very best anesthesiologists in the region was occasionally slipped in to tend to some very rich patients. When Erlanger finally agreed to employ black doctors there, there was only one who could qualify to serve at the hospital. But after state certifications were satisfied, two more qualified. In 1963, the first black surgeon operated at Erlanger. Later on, we were able to get a black woman to head the hospitals' housekeeping division, and in the 1980s we aided in elevating Mr. Irvin Overton to the second highest position in the Erlanger Health system. For an interim period, he even served as acting CEO. After Mr. Overton was promoted, there was a noticeable increase in the number of black physicians, not only in the hospital but all throughout the city.

INVESTIGATING HIRING PRACTICES

The Tennessee Valley Authority (the TVA) is a government agency established in the 1930s to bring electricity to much of the south. We commissioned a study which showed that blacks constituted some 32 percent of the population in the TVA region of operation. I joined with two TVA employees - James Steele (who was president of the Huntsville Alabama branch of the NAACP and Monroe Powers (president of the South Pittsburg, Tennessee branch) to do an in-house study regarding TVA's employment practices. Since I did not work for TVA, it was my lot to lead the way and we found that the TVA had a very poor record of hiring blacks despite federal affirmative action mandates established in 1961.

Our committee exposed racism at practically all areas of its operation. We found that there were vast patterns of racial discrimination in most areas of the company. Whites with only minimal skills and very little education could get good paying jobs while blacks with college degrees were limited to janitorial service and mailroom supervision. But thanks to our persistence, jobs in other areas eventually became available to black workers.

In the 1970s, the TVA had some 5,600 employees in the Chattanooga area with less than 1% who were black. Some contractors had almost no blacks working, even though there was a federal mandate in place. As the TVA started building its $200 million headquarters building in Chattanooga, I sought to get 10% set aside to allow Black owned companies like my own to provide insurance coverage. But with my entry, the TVA decided to self-insure rather than let me bid on covering some of its policies.

As late as the 1990s, I served on the Human Relations Committee of the TVA and continued to call their attention to the disparities. It would be 2006 before any blacks served on the TVA board of directors.

We also investigated hiring practices of the federal courts in the Eastern District of Tennessee. In 1996, there were only four blacks employed in the entire Eastern District: two women in the Bankruptcy Court of Chattanooga, U.S. Attorney Curtis Collier and David Jennings, who was the first black probation officer. All were housed in Chattanooga. I shared this information with Vice President Al Gore. Not long after, Attorney Collier was elevated to federal judge and later to Chief judge.

From 1975 to '78 I served two years as president of the State Conference of Branches of the NAACP. State Representative C.B.

Robinson made appointments with the governor for me to discuss our NAACP initiatives for the year and to seek his help in carrying them out.

Working through our senator, I discovered that the federal government was the Tennessee's largest employer and I was able to get annual reports on federal employment. Departments such as the Air Force had no blacks, while others there were only token hirings. I shared this information with other branches within the state in the hope that they could use it to create avenues of employment advancement.

For many years I worked to secure more hiring and promotions with the Tennessee Highway Patrol. In 1977 there were 650 state trooper troopers while blacks numbered only 13, with only one ever having the rank of Sergeant. I worked on behalf of Trooper James Cunningham from his days as a patrolman until he became the first black captain. In Chattanooga, I pushed to get blacks hired in the Driver's License division and was successful.

Over the years there have been moderate gains from the early days to the point where blacks have climbed the ladder to serve in top positions of some agencies. However, it was apparent that while proclaiming equal opportunity the federal government failed to carry out affirmative action mandates in many areas.

The Hamilton County government remained very segregated racially in terms of elected offices and county jobs. I challenged the various departments of county government to open the doors to employment, but there seems to be little concern at the county level when it comes to hiring Blacks.

Except for the city of Chattanooga, Hamilton County had–as late as 2007– fifteen judges with no black having ever served as an elected or appointed county judge. This has been one area in which we have struggled for years without results. Certainly, with all–white judgeships, the proportion of blacks being sentenced is reflective of systemic racism.

I would admonish the city on such things as using the employees of the Chattanooga Housing Authority, which was a private agency contracting with the city, to meet their affirmative action goals.

I believe it is important that we, as a people recognize that there is no point where everything remains the same. Although reaping the fruit of those who labored long and hard, few seem to feel the obligation or responsibility to keep the doors open for others. For progress to become permanent, there has to be a reckoning of how one got their position, an honesty in realizing that they did not make it on their own and a commitment to hold open the door they just passed through. Doing unto others must be the first rule of permanent advancement.

Since our trials began in this country so long ago we find our greatest success in being a communal people who put others like themselves first. When we lose that sense of community and decide to go it on our own, we become targets to be picked off one by one. I don't know why this is such a hard lesson to grasp, but I will continue to seek opportunity and advantage whenever and wherever I can for my people.

**Hundreds Jam Church to Honor Mapps for
Courage and Commitment to Rights**
MR. AND MRS. JAMES R. MAPP are joined on the front row at Orchard Knob Missionary Baptist Church by three of their daughters. Thirty-one other family members, including 14 grandchildren, sit in the rows behind them [photo caption]. They called him a man with a vision—a man who had the courage to stand alone and put his life on the line to help others. *The Chattanooga Times* archives, April 20, 1987.

CHAPTER 11
The Long Road To School Desegregation

THE ROAD THROUGH THE COURTS IN the school segregation lawsuit was long and arduous. The Supreme Court decision in Brown Versus the Board of Education in 1954 stated that desegregation should come "with all deliberate speed". While on the surface it seems to be a clear statement, the Court left plenty of room in allowing local school jurisdictions to determine what "deliberate speed" meant. In Chattanooga it meant "proceed at your own rate" and we would find out that "deliberate speed" in desegregation would take a total of 26 years.

This gave some white churches time to set up so-called "Christian schools" designed to avoid being subjected to desegregation. This not only meant to include long-standing churches or private schools, rather those fly-by-night church schools whose sole purpose was to separate the races.

During the court proceedings, outdated editions of textbooks were still being used in black schools as late as the 1980s. The reason the school officials gave was that black teachers preferred these editions. This was a lie. The great shortage of textbooks in the Negro schools could be traced to the Board of Education sharing newer edition textbooks with the recently set up church schools.

In 1960 the case was entered on the court docket as James Jonathan Mapp et al. v. the Chattanooga-Board of Education. Although the case was in my son's name, our daughter Deborah L'Tanya Mapp was also a plaintiff.

At the beginning of the litigation, three parents (Mrs. Josephine Maxey, the Reverend H. H. Kirnon, and myself) were in attendance. Shortly after the suit started, Mrs. Maxey married and moved from Chattanooga, then Kirnon was transferred to a different church outside of Chattanooga. This left me as the only litigant.

At the time of the Brown decision, the schools in the city of Chattanooga and its surrounding Hamilton County were two separate systems, While it took a lawsuit to get the city to start the desegregation process, the county voluntarily desegregated after Rev. Frank S. Walker, and I went to the central office and requested admission for his two children at Lookout Mountain Elementary school. The county opened up immediately. This prevented city students from turning to the county system as a segregated safe haven.

In 1962 the first stages of court ordered desegregation began at the elementary school level. Our daughter, Angela, was in the first group enrolled at Sunnyside Elementary. Many had predicted trouble, but none occurred. The day was quiet and peaceful as the handful of black students entered the formally all-white school. City police were assigned to Sunnyside "to keep the peace" but no pro segregation crowds gathered and with the exception of a few new students in attendance, the day proceeded like any other.

School Change Orderly ...

Children Leave Glenwood School After Registering [photo caption] Limited desegregation in the first three grades at selected schools was started Wednesday under federal court directive ... Officials said the people of the community responded with a dignity and respect for law and order. *Chattanooga Daily Times* archives, August 30, 1962.

The gradual process of desegregation caused the Mapp family to have to continue participating in segregated schools for another five years before Vi and I got seven of our eight children into integrated schools in the Brainerd area of the city. Meanwhile, our four older children still had to be taken five miles across Missionary Ridge to school. Our oldest daughter, Brenda, was the only one to graduate in 1966 from an all black Riverside High School. Riverside, formerly Chattanooga High had been assigned to Negro students in 1962 as the second Negro high school in the city.

Our second daughter, Deborah, and third daughter Michaellee, got the opportunity to enroll in the newly desegregated Brainerd High School in 1967 and our oldest son, Jonathan, was enrolled at Brainerd Junior High. With Brenda now off to college, this would mark the first time all seven of our children at home would be attending school in the Brainerd area where we lived.

Through the years of litigation, very few from the black community came to the courtroom during the hearings and trial. In the 1970's it was discomforting to see both blacks and whites on the side of the school board although some, like Commissioner Of Education John P. Franklin (elected in 1971), privately lamented being on the opposite side. He was Chattanooga's first elected black of that rank in 60 years and as commissioner was chairman of the school board. Although fate had placed us on differing sides, from time-to-time Johnny Franklin had encouraging words for me as he knew the case persisted at great cost to my family, my peace of mind and financial security. He understood how long and hard was the row I had to hoe.

Our attorneys were excellent, and our expert witnesses did a very credible job due to the efficiency of Attorney Constance Baker Motley who had argued so eloquently in many similar cases. Judge Frank Wilson seemed to enjoy the competency of our attorneys and at times appeared to be in awe of Nashville attorney Mr. Avon Williams. A casual observer would have thought that our case was "open and shut" by way of arguments. But this being the old South, the good-old-boy network sought to protect the status quo by stretching the case out rather than dealing directly with the issue at hand. Not only did our attorneys have to overcome a zealous defense council, they often had to also deal with this judge who constantly bent over backwards to find ways to make the school board attorneys look more competent.

At one point in the trial the court presented an expense account to me. Normally it was not necessary for the plaintiff to sign for expenses of the attorneys but the judge made me sign before paying the small stipend of about $9,000. We felt this was yet another tactic to intimidate us because we were winning the case. In that courtroom the pursuit of justice ran second to the preservation of old Southern ways. The court had used every conceivable means to delay the decision. But in the end, they had no other choice but to rule in our favor.

In the early days of the suit, as I sat in the courtroom and listened to the presentation of the case, I felt that there was no way that our attorneys had not won on our behalf. But this thought would soon disappear when the judges cut down the great efforts of our legal team. The strange thing is that Judge Wilson's demeanor on the bench did not conform to his rulings. Anyone entering the courtroom for a short visit would have been impressed by him and had the feeling he was just and fair, but that was not the case. He had been assigned to the court from upper East Tennessee and this immediately raised a question of whether he would act in a manner consistent with the extreme conservatism of that section of the state.

The strategy of sending black women attorneys to the South perhaps confused both the court and opposing counsel. And because of their knowledge and skill it was very difficult for the opposing counsel, who time and again seemed to rely on his "whiteness" rather than his legal arguments.

One day, while sitting in the courtroom, I looked at the painted mural on the wall. It depicted black slaves in the field working. I also took note that the entire staff was white. I was moved to write a letter to the editor of the Times about it and questioned whether or not there could be any fairness or justice in a courtroom that accepted the attitude that nothing was wrong with that mural. Apparently, some official took note of my letter and not long after a black young man became the first hired by that court.

As each circumstance presented itself, I would try to make issues function more smoothly. Because of my familiarity with the system, I wrote many notes to my attorneys to counter the approaches that the opposition would use. I made sure that the counsel was keenly aware of the inner operation of the school system. I educated them on all of the maneuvering, misstatements, and total fabrications already presented. I kept in touch with the attorneys even when we were not in court. As a result they filed motion after motion keeping the superintendent, school hoard, and their attorney very very busy.

The school board attorneys were taken aback by some of the challenges in the court where established norms were not followed. Attorney Motley had presented our case as precedent setting. It was a deviation from other cases on school desegregation. Our suit was allowed to be broadened to include as plaintiffs teachers, principals and other Board of Education personnel who had regular contact with students. This move was important in protecting any witnesses from losing their jobs during the trial.

From time to time as desegregation was taking place, it was necessary for the branch to come to the aid of students at Brainerd High and Central High schools. Parents were fearful that the children were being mistreated by other students, the police, and the school. The parents asked the NAACP to intervene. At one point we had to use the services of Attorney Avon Williams of Nashville to defend students arrested at Brainerd High School.

It was also during that time that a group of black Brainerd residents joined me in meeting with what turned out to be a white citizens' council. The meeting was held in the basement of a store on Brainerd Road and there was standing room only. Some fifteen or so of us Blacks showed up thinking that the meeting was intended for all residents of the Brainerd area, as it was announced in the newspaper "Brainerd citizens concerning Brainerd High School." It did not take long for us to realize what the meeting was all about.

White parents began to recount what happened to their children. At this point someone yelled from the audience, "They are not with us, and they should leave." The crowd began get very restless, whereupon the chairman said, "These people have caused no disturbance and they have a right to be here." At this point I sensed real danger and announced, "We will leave because we do not want to disturb your meeting."

The next day a detective from the Chattanooga Police Department, who was assigned to the meeting, related to me that we had no idea what could have happened. Those people were armed to the hilt. The police department had expected trouble, so a number of plain clothes officers were in the crowd.

The detective said it was good we had left when we did. But as African American parents we demonstrated the level of concern for all children by our willingness to take risks on their behalf. We were willing to look into and discuss whatever, whenever and however if the primary goal was to find solutions.

Before the desegregation plan was fully implemented, many white students had left Brainerd High, and by the late 1970s it was practically all black. And although all of our children were out of the house or off to college Vi and I became co-presidents of the PTA. As the National Parent Teacher Association (PTA) endorsed racially integrated education in the 1970s, local whites set up what they called the (PTO) the Parent Teacher organization. They explained the reason for this as "keeping the money at, home." Rather than supporting the national PTA- which had taken a stand on endorsing integration - they defected.

In the thirteenth year of the ongoing law suit the school board offered a plan that the court accepted. The plan called for reassigning teachers in a manner to greater reflect the student population, which through busing was 60 percent white and 40 percent black. The school board plan was accepted by the court in 1973 and was referred to as a full desegregation plan. The plan however, allowed for many loopholes in the majority-to-minority transfer provisions. Our attorneys sought to seek relief from these ambiguities through the appeals process but to no avail.

Because of the systematic disenfranchisement of the Chattanooga public school system, in 1979 Brainerd High school was looked upon as being one of the worst in the Chattanooga Public School System. We parents strategized with Dr. Colbert Whitaker (the principal), who did a great job in reversing the problems. Together we secured half page ads in the Chattanooga Times touting good things that were happening in the school. By 1981 Brainerd Senior High School had more national merit scholars than any other high school in the city, including private schools. This shows what can be done when all are willing to row in the same direction.

Year after year we petitioned the court for reliefs noting that the school board attorney sought every possible delay. At the end of the court litigation in 1986, a number of events took place that would radically change the makeup of the Chattanooga school system.

Black male teachers and principals were demoted and dismissed at an alarming rate. Black teachers, who had tenure were given the option to retire by using strong financial incentives. Seasoned black teachers who remained were transferred to predominantly white schools.

The plan as presented by the black parents and attorneys:

The school board's desegregation plan called for a 60 percent white to 40 percent black teacher ratio in all schools. Our attorneys opposed this plan and offered a plan that would require 60 percent white and 40 percent black teachers in majority white schools, and 60 percent black and 40 percent white teachers in majority black schools. The school board objected to our plan, and the court sided with the school board.

In 1989, sixteen schools in Chattanooga were closed without adequate planning. Of the schools closed, fourteen had black principals. The reason given was budgetary concerns. Another ruse was to have a Reconfiguration Committee formed. The committee closed schools by saying that they were in poor condition. This was still another lie. Schools that were slated to close were somehow deemed salvageable once they were emptied. Then they were put back into service. None of the black principals were given lateral movement and appointed to these schools. All were demoted, whereas the two white principals got lateral movement.

Under the leadership of Mayor Gene Roberts the city abandoned public education and left the responsibility for educating Chattanooga's children to the predominately white county school system.

Before the city ceded Chattanooga's public education to county control 40 percent of the teachers were black. When the county took over, the new Chattanooga Hamilton County school system had less than 8 percent black teachers.

In 1987 the twenty-six-year-old desegregation suit was closed. In the end, did we win? Technically yes. But for all intent and purpose, it is debatable whether the education for black students in Chattanooga was for the better.

I'm telling you...No matter how hard you try... when it comes to people willing to do anything to hold onto their long-held beliefs and advantages—it seems that sometimes you just can't win for losing.

CHAPTER 12
Persistence: Enduring the Hardships

BEING A CIVIL RIGHTS LEADER DID not come without its problems. My family and I have endured misfortune along the way, but through it all we continued to be persistent and pressed on to do what we felt needed to be done.

Early in the 1960s, sugar was placed in the tank of my car. Fortunately, I discovered what was happening in time, and Mr. Andrew Jackson was able to clean out the engine before the sugar totally destroyed it. Through the years, Mr. Jackson had not only been the dealer whom I bought cars, but a friend and a great supporter. When things were often rough financially, he would always come through for me, and in fact he was the reason I could stay in business. When it appeared that I could not go on, he was there to help. I shall always remember and appreciate Mr. Jackson. In 2003 he saw me catching the bus because my car had broken down. He called me to his lot and gave me a 1995 Chrysler and paid all transfer costs. He's the kind of man who helped many in this town who had troubles. Many times it seemed that he could sense when I was in trouble and he would come by the office and offer help.

Although in his 90s, Mr. Jackson was civically active and still sells cars from his lot. It wasn't uncommon to see him working on cars. Mr. Jackson has been in business for sixty-five years –longer than anyone else on Martin Luther King Junior Blvd. He was the first black person to serve on the Planning Commission of Chattanooga. Like many others, he got his start driving a taxi on what was called the Jitney Line, a Negro taxi service. There are not many true friends like Mr. Jackson. One of his sons went into the ministry and the other one joined him in his father's business.

The school suit led to many trying days and experiences that would tax my family to the limits. In 1962 the bank where I did business stopped lending me money. Earlier, because of my good credit, I could walk into the bank and get a signature loan of $1,000 or more. Later, my wife had to come and sign with me. This lasted a short time until the banker asked me to bring my wife and another person to co-sign with us. Mr. James L. Jenkins signed a couple of loans but after that was told by the bank, "We will lend to you the money and you can lend it to Mr. Mapp". This certainly infuriated Mr. Jenkins and ended my ability to borrow at that bank. Another financial institution (where the manager was white) let me continue to borrow despite the school suit.

I had worked for a large well-established insurance company for fifteen years. My manager, Mr. Grady H. Harris, fended off calls and threats designed to make me lose my job. Mr. Harris stood by me, and I suspect that this is why the company transferred him to the Chicago District. When his replacement arrived, I immediately sensed that he was to be the hatchet man. Sure enough, he demoted me from staff manager to a debit collector because they said I was spending too much time in court. One would have thought that I was protected by a Negro-owned company, but in the end this was not the case.

After the court case was filed, many calls came to the district office of my employer demanding that I be fired. They said things such as "Fire that nigger" and more. Calls were made to my home day and night, some threatening. Since the other two litigants no longer lived in town, I was the single target. Some wanted to know where Carroll Street was - that's where we lived. I directed them to Carroll Lane in North Chattanooga, even though we lived on the east side of town. Carroll Street was only one block long. Everyone in the neighborhood knew me since I lived within one block of Carroll some twenty-five years. This was comforting.

Viola, my wife, was a real trooper in that she took everything in stride. I had previously warned her to not come see me if she got a call that something had happened. I emphasized that she was not to come, but send someone because she might be used as bait to get me if she was taken into custody or kidnapped. At night we would let the telephone stay on until we got tired of the constant ringing. We would then take the phone off the hook until the next morning. During the entire ordeal we never had our telephone number changed although there were constant threats on our lives.

Vi had our children under control and would not let them answer the phone. Much of what was told to her over the phone was kept from me for years. Because of her fearlessness, the children stayed calm. Our youngest daughter was born in 1960 at the height of the threats with a nervous twitch of her head, which she soon outgrew. I wondered if this was related to the stress we were under.

Initially I armed myself as I rode around in the car after the school suit was filed and the sit-ins started. After a few days I decided I would not be armed. I thought that no having my pistol handy would cause me to think rather than react if provoked.

Today I am glad I made that decision. Early on I became very cautious and was careful about the routes that I took, being ever mindful that there were a number of die-hards who would delight in my demise. Even today I can't help but have flashes of those times, and this still keeps me on my toes.

During that time we were blessed in that many men, some of whom I did not know, voluntarily came by to guard our house at night and provide protection for my family. They were Mr. John Winston Simpson (my roommate at Tennessee A&I State University), the Reverend Oscar Lockhart, Mr. Ralph Thomas, the two Morgan brothers, the Reverend Buford McElrath, Mr. Emmit Walker, and others. These men demonstrated concern and commitment. They assured me that our family would be safe as desegregation efforts were under way.

Some would come as soon as it got dark and stay until the eleven o'clock shift got off and then they would stay til morning. These men asked nothing of us but were willing to give their service to protect my family. Most of them were quiet family men and we are forever indebted to them. A city police officer (Mr. Walter Maples) often stood guard after his shift was over. These were men who believed that strides toward freedom should not be stifled.

When I worked for the Model Cities Program, there was a lot of pressure on me because of my job, the pressures of my production, and trying to keep my own insurance business open at the same time. I was the only entry-level employee at Model Cities who had to be hired by the entire city commission. It appeared that the city leadership did not know what to do with me and had no choice but to hire me after talking to such people as Mr. C. B. Robinson.

As president of the local branch of the NAACP, I would not sacrifice my obligation to the branch to appease the city. I led the branch in filing a suit against the city, while on payroll, that ruled in favor of a Model Cities Program resident. I took on the Chattanooga Housing Authority and the Urban Renewal Project when they attempted to use programs against the citizens of the model and urban renewal neighborhoods.

While I served as president of the NAACP state conference, I lost my job with Model Cities and had very little income. I remember traveling more than three hundred miles to meet with a branch in the tri-cities area in northwest Tennessee. The small branch could only give me $25 dollars toward gas, but they gave my wife and me a very good meal. I left Chattanooga early in the morning, arrived there before the scheduled time of the program and returned to Chattanooga immediately afterward so that there would not be a hotel bill. The state conference also had very little money and could not afford a night's lodging. In spite of the circumstances, it was a very enjoyable trip.

In 1971 Vi and I went to an NAACP convention in Minneapolis, Minnesota. We left some of our children with our relatives in Springfield, Ohio. We drove all night to make the thousand-mile journey for the opening of the convention on Monday. We made the trip successfully, attended the session, and planned to get a good night's sleep. Our older son, who had stayed at home, went out on a date that Monday night—the Fourth of July. He stayed late and, as fate would have it, returned to find that our home had been bombed. The damage was under his and his brother's bedroom. As soon as my son saw the damage, he called us to let us know what had happened. That was one time that we were glad that he had stayed out late.

As soon as day broke we left the convention to return home. After driving the thousand miles the day before, I drove all but fifty miles, when Vi took over. I took little rest during the long trip back home and was very tired. On returning, we found that the back of the house had been heavily damaged under the boys' room near the kitchen. We were fortunate in that the blast of the heavy charge of dynamite projected out rather than upward and total destruction was averted. Our neighbor, Mr. Grover Fryar, a retired military man (who happened to be white), lived across the street. His specialty in the army was explosives, and he said that we were blessed that the thick rock wall of the basement caused the dynamite to project outward rather than upward. This would have destroyed the entire house.

Our insurance provided only a part of what was needed to make repairs. The bombing caused us to make some changes to update our home. The walls of our home were plaster and the blast made it necessary for us to put sheetrock throughout the entire house except one bedroom. This also gave us an opportunity to add two bedrooms and a bath. All ten of us had previously used one bath without a shower, but over the years we somehow had made it work. At this time three of our children were in college, and it was a welcome relief to have two bathrooms when they came home. We even added a partially finished basement for the younger children to play.

When the delegates at the NAACP convention heard about what had happened to us, they decided to forego any parties and sent us some $900 to help us make our home livable. My hometown of Chattanooga, including my church, gave us no assistance. The only exceptions were Mr. Levi Moore, who gave us twenty-five dollars and Mr. Roy Noel, who gave us twenty. The local NAACP branch did nothing in the way of support, and I am not sure my own church even prayed for us. We were disappointed but we continued to support both the branch and our church. We were, as usual, continuing to work on behalf of our people.

During this time a number of other bombings took place in Chattanooga, but the police failed to apprehend anyone. I recall that the home of Mr. and Mrs. Thomas Reed was bombed in St. Elmo. They later became strong supporters of the NAACP, working for many years with the Youth Council locally, statewide and nationally. The home of Reverend A.M. Syler on Dodds Avenue was also bombed during this period of time. The Reverend Syler was pastor of the Friendship Primitive Baptist Church.

I believe that it was in the 1980s that I received a call from a man in Rossville, Georgia who said he wanted me to list a property on Dodson Avenue. I went out and viewed the property. It a very nice piece of land. I called him and set an appointment for one in the afternoon. It was about eleven in the morning when I called to confirm the appointment. I decided to ask Mr. Jesse Houston, an affiliate broker, to go with me on this listing. Normally I would have not asked anyone to accompany me, but I had an eerie feeling that caused me to ask, or maybe it was just a protective guardian angel that led me in this direction.

Mr. Houston worked full-time as a guard and was still wearing his guard uniform, including his pistol. As we arrived at the address just across the Tennessee line in Georgia, we found a junk car lot. As I entered, I saw a couple of unsavory looking guys strolling the lot with their eyes on me. I got out of the car and entered the building and what seemed to be an office. Mr. Houston, in the meantime, got out and was standing beside the car with his pistol in view on his side. The man with whom I had the appointment had a pistol lying on his desk. After he looked out and saw Houston, he said to me, "I have just sold that property." And that was only two hours after I had confirmed the appointment.

Every instinct in me said this was a setup that intended to cause me harm. My feeling was that I had been lured there, perhaps for a lynching. The property they allegedly wanted to sell continued to have the For Sale sign up many months later. To this day I believe that had I been alone, I would have been the victim of a lynch party.

Desegregation Suit Took Mapps on a Lonely Voyage of Principle and Danger
Mapp is a quiet, dignified man who—despite what he's been through, or maybe because of it—seems to have inner peace. He has his own insurance and real estate agency, a sparsely furnished storefront office in a section of stores and bars on Martin Luther King Jr. Boulevard. His artful, almost scholarly conversation and his appearance—wire rimmed glasses, herringbone wool tweed jacket—make him seem more an educator than a businessman. *The Chattanooga Times* archives, February 9, 1987.

To accommodate those who had to work and could not come down to the NAACP office during working hours, I would open the office on Saturday and sometimes on Sunday. I often worked virtually alone while at the same time trying to find a way to make my insurance and real estate business profitable again. In 2006 I continued to come to the office daily with the expectation that I would make a good sale and put myself in a position to retire.

As a family we did not have money, but we served unselfishly and were inwardly rewarded. We felt that God had blessed us with an unusual gift that we freely shared over the many years. In her later years while undergoing cancer treatment, Vi still gave to the extent that her health would allow, even to the end.

I constantly think of how important all our children were to us. I guess that had a lot to do the actions we took and why we could replace fear with action and find a kind of beauty in sacrifice. As I grow older and look back on their childhood at what many would call poverty conditions, I see great beauty and serenity in the life we lived. I especially note the contributions my late wife and I both made because of the many chances we took and how we used every circumstance to make things better in our community, city, state and nation.

We all had a deep and abiding faith in God
and feared doing nothing
more than doing something.

CHAPTER 13

The Family

A LOVE STORY

I BELIEVE THAT INDUSTRIOUSNESS, SELF-RELIANCE AND INDEPENDENCE from both families was handed down from the past generations and shaped the way Vi and I chose to see our place as citizens in this society.

Vi and I were a great partnership. Not only in the traditional sense as husband and wife – but as the years went by, we acted as equals in an unequal society. I would take pleasure in watching her grow from a dedicated housewife and mother to a civic and community leader in her own right.

Whenever one would lead, the other would follow and support. Our children, for the most part, took on these same kinds of traits and now exhibit them before their children. I am happy to say that all of our children seem to be thoughtful of others and free of feelings of inferiority. All show a depth of sympathy and are willing to give of themselves.

Aside from the generation that preceded my father, I do not have much record of his side of the family. My father's father was Alfred Mapp. It was said that he had roots in Barbados and his father was a slave who accompanied General James Oglethorpe when he first settled Georgia in the 1700s. Alfred's wife, my grandmother, was Ida

Ruff Mapp whose relatives were very fair skinned, although she was dark of complexion. Alfred and Ida had six children one of whom was James Albert Mapp, my father.

Of my father's family, the Hargroves of Hancock County Georgia, Israel Hargrove my great grandfather was full-blooded Cherokee who lived to be between 106 and 110 years old. His occupation was hunting and fishing. He married a former slave named Amanda (Mandy), who bore Henry, my grandfather. Henry married Elnora Brundage, my grandmother and she birthed my mother, Mattie Lou who was the ninth of their ten children.

My father, James Albert Mapp and my mother Mattie Lou Hargrove were wed in 1926. They had two children, me, James Rogers Mapp and my sister Mary Elizabeth Mapp. While they were estranged due to spousal abuse, my father died of tuberculosis and pneumonia in 1930.

Of my wife Viola, her mother's family were the Tutts Their white relations and surname originated in Ireland. They came to America during the Revolutionary War. They settled first in Virginia before moving to Elkton, Kentucky. Her grandfather, Marcellus Tutt was the first generation of Tutts born after slavery. He married Cynthia Jane Allison, the daughter of a white doctor and a Negro woman. Marcellus and Cynthia Jane had six children, one of which was Vi's mother, Beatrice.

Vi's family on her father's side are the Martins, an extraordinary family in Western Kentucky. More of them later.

Was it chance or circumstance that a country boy from the heart of Georgia would meet a country girl from Kentucky in the state of Tennessee? It seems improbable given that in those who lived in rural Black southern areas at that time, generally lived their entire lives close to the communities of their birth. But times were changing and after World War II, many Negroes abandoned the south for what they considered to be "freedom in the North." Hundreds of thousands of Negroes headed north to escape the terrors of Jim Crow laws and segregation. They joined the black migration movement to cities like Chicago, Detroit, Pittsburg and New York.

In some ways my Vi and I had similar backgrounds. We came from respected families with good names. We knew farm life intimately. But the difference was that my first years were in the hills of Georgia on a poor one-horse farm, one step up from being a sharecropper – while Vi was raised on a large property that had been owned by her family since 1848, seventeen years before the end of slavery.

We were both good students who walked the dusty roads of the countryside in our elementary school years. While I attended a make-shift school in a small log Baptist church, Vi attended a state-of-the-art Rosenwald-built school. It was constructed specifically for the small Negro farming community of Rhodes chapel – that was populated by a couple dozen or so Black families.

For those who don't know, Rosenwald Schools were a project initiated by Tuskegee Institute founder Booker T. Washington and financed by philanthropist and president of Sears Roebuck and Company, Julius Rosenwald of Chicago. Almost five thousand schools were built across the south. By 1928 they served an estimated one-third of the South's rural black children.

Vi's family, the Martins, was an example of what Negroes could become if given a chance. Her great grandfather Lourenza Dow Martin was an enslaved man who was recognized as the son of his master. This is the probable reason that as an adult he got the opportunity to purchase his freedom in 1848 and two years later purchased freedom for his wife, Minnie Malvina Reynolds. At the same time Lourenza bought a hundred acres of land and later purchased another 149. Lourenza and Melvina bore a son named Finis, who married Willie Mathis. Finis and Willie bore a son named Herbert who was Viola's father and who became my father-in-law.

While I never knew my own father, Vi's father, Herbert Leslie Martin was a rarity. He was a third generation Negro farmer in a predominantly white southern farming region. Mr. Martin was the only sibling of his generation who chose to embrace farm life. The others opted for town and city life mostly in Ohio. Mr. Martin as I called him, initially purchased one hundred acres from his father. Over the years his farm did well as he added property to grow what was to become at its peak, about twelve hundred acres. It was one of the largest farms in Western Kentucky.

The farm, still owned by the family to this day is said to have the highest point in the county. The family called the high point Bald Knob Hill while those whites who were envious referred to it as "Nigger Hill." Bald Knob Hill descends into a fertile valley of soil -rich acres called "bottom land." The valley was the heart of what came to be known as Martin acres.

Mr. Martin and his wife Beatrice, better known as "Momma Bea," became prosperous Negro farmers during the same time my own grandfather's farm was stolen by white racists. Herbert Martin was one of those fellows with straight hair and a straight narrow nose who kind of looked like a white man with a deep tan. But there was no doubt that when it came to claiming his heritage, Mr. Martin was what we called back then, a proud "race Man." I am sure in color-struck America his light complexion and looks helped him in business matters with his white neighbors, as they somehow felt more comfortable dealing with a person who looked like them.

I find it amazing how Mr. Martin was able to hold onto valuable property that had deposits of coal, oil, natural gas and timber. Armed only with a sixth-grade education, my father-in-law was a well-spoken man. A constant reader, he was up on current events his entire life. Throughout the years there were efforts to disrupt his success. But he was a careful businessman who paid his taxes on time and dotted all "I's" and crossed all "T's." This earned him respect even from those detractors who felt that no Negro should have so much. Herbert Martin was an exceptional man.

For a Black man to be an upward striver in the south invited a target on his back. Black success could breed open hostility from less successful whites. Given the racial climate of the country, when there were record numbers of lynchings and race riot, Mr. Martin was one who readily protected himself and his kin. He dealt with would-be detractors firmly and let his mind be known in no uncertain terms. He commanded respect and respect was given.

Most of all he treated all who he encountered with neighborly kindness. He was a friend to the local farmer, both black and white and he was always there to lend his neighbor a tool, some machinery, advice or help. Being one of the first with modern farm equipment, Mr. Martin would lend it freely or lease it at a minimal amount. Before the rural electric movement gave family farms in Muhlenberg county electric power in the 1950s, the Martins were one of the first to have a battery powered radio in the area in the 1930's. It was a common sight on Saturday nights for neighbors – both Black and white – to gather at what was referred to as the "big house" to listen to the Grand Ole Opry.

Such generosity went a long way in diluting racial animosity. While it would be foolish to think that generations of racial segregation no longer existed, or that in their "heart of hearts" white neighbors still clung to the idea of racial superiority, the unwritten law of "neighbor helping neighbor" trumped many prejudices. So much so that in 1965 Herbert Martin, a Colored man in an overwhelmingly white county, ran on the republican ticket for magistrate and lost by only a handful of votes. That's how much respect he had garnered over the years.

As time passed, Mr. Martin and I grew to have mutual respect for one another. We talked about politics regularly. He was what you call a lifelong "Lincolnian Republican." Many Blacks only a few decades from slavery still identified and voted for the party of whom they considered to be the Great Emancipator. For the most part, I considered myself an independent. I mostly voted democrat but there were the few occasions I voted Republican. Some might be surprised that in 1960 I voted for Richard Nixon. At the time, Senator Kennedy avoided the race controversy and offered no solutions or legislation. Nixon, on the other had did have a track record, all be it small regarding inclusion and benefits for the Black race. Just let it be said that the Nixon of 1960 was a far cry from the conservative Nixon of '68 and 72. Both times I voted democrat for Humphrey and then McGovern.

Mr. Martin was somewhat conservative. He was a self-made man who believed that folks shouldn't depend on the government and could pull themselves up by their own bootstraps. I, on the other hand believed in social programs designed to help the many. Of our many discussions - or should I say debates - we respected one another's opinions and occasionally saw eye to eye. But he did once compliment me by saying to one of my kids, "when it comes to your daddy.... I never met anyone who has a greater faith in the good of human nature."

As friends, neighbors, and relations, the Martins, past and present were and are the best of people. As I said before, Vi's family is an example of what Negroes could become if only given a chance.

COLLEGE AND COURTSHIP

At age ten, I left Georgia for good. Mother opted for city life, raising Sister and me in Chattanooga. Vi got a chance to leave the farm after graduating from the all-colored Drakesboro high school in Muhlenberg County Kentucky. A cousin-educator of her father named Hume Mathis convinced him to send Vi and her older sister Ernestine to college. The objective was not only for an education but to also increase the chance of Herbert's daughters meeting and marrying educated young Colored men with a future.

Fortunately for Vi and me, racial situations where we lived – while bad, weren't so dire. There was a Negro institution of higher learning located in Nashville, Tennessee – Midway between Chattanooga and Vi's hometown of Greenville. After high school we both attend what was then called Tennessee Agriculture and Industrial State College, or Tennessee A and I. In 1968 it would become known as Tennessee State University.

As a result of the injury to my hand at the age of six, my sister Mary and I were a half year apart in school and we both graduated with honors. I always maintained that she was a better student than I was because she studied harder. I graduated as president and valedictorian of the class of 1947 and Mary was an honor student. Sister got married right after graduation. I really wanted her to go to college, however, she and Mother insisted that I go instead.

During my first year at Tennessee A&I State College, I ran for president of the class. I didn't win but apparently made enough of an impression to be elected vice president.

After being on campus for some six weeks, I met Viola Martin for the first time. One Sunday afternoon her sister Ernestine (who was dating my roommate Tom Jenkins) was walking on campus with two other girls when I saw one I thought I'd like to date. I asked Ernestine to sign out, and we went off campus with Tom. At that time freshmen girls had to sign out in fours. The girl I had planned to talk to was walking arm in arm with another girl, so I fell in line with the one who was walking behind, a girl named Viola. I was impressed with her beauty as we sat in the booth at Price's restaurant. The sun shone through her chestnut-colored hair, and in no time flat I was hooked.

Vi and I were good students while at A&I State College. My background from junior high school served me well, as did my high school training. And I was even able to assist my college English teacher, who was a recent graduate. I also participated in the Little Theater while there. Our drama teacher wanted a girl she like get close to me, but I already had met Vi and there was no contest. Another girl form Mississippi showed a lot of interest in me, but I was taken.

After our first date I went to my dorm that night and wrote to Mother, describing Vi in a most tender way. I was hooked and so was she, and after that we would always be seen together. After classes we had dinner and would go the recreation hall and dance to the song "Since I fell for You."

Working hard since age twelve, I had saved some money and hoped I could make it through the first year without working. I fared well until the last of January when my stepfather got sick. It took every dollar Mother made to take care of things at home. It was then I wrote to my uncle Harry in New York. He had bragged about what he was going to do for my sister and me, so I asked him for a twenty-five-dollar loan until I could get out of school for the summer. He had no children, owned a three-story flat in the Bronx, and had a very successful dry-cleaning business in Harlem. I never heard from him. I became so poor that I could not buy a nickel bar of soap or a three-cent stamp.

I was able to get registered for the second semester because my stepfather was back at work, and my mother could share some money with me. Tuition, room, and board were $115 for in-state students. I only had a few dollars left and decided to venture off campus, renting a room which cost only a dollar per week. During the time that I was financially down, Vi would take my clothes to her dorm and wash them for me.

Vi became pregnant during our freshman year. I immediately asked her to marry me, and she agreed. When we were out for the summer, I wrote to her father to ask for her hand in marriage. Mr. Martin who was wary of "city slickers" wrote back and said, "I would advise you, young man, to stay down there in Chattanooga." Being young and in love, I would not let this response satisfy me.

After his letter we decided that I would visit Vi's home in Greenville, Kentucky. I left Chattanooga about eleven thirty on Saturday night. arriving in Greenville about nine o'clock Sunday morning. I caught a Yellow Cab to the road that led to her family farm and then I walked about a mile. Vi waited for me under a big oak tree about a quarter mile from her house. The tree was in an open field but still hidden away from the road. She brought us a very good picnic lunch and I stayed with her until it was time to catch my 3:30 bus back home. I arrived in Chattanooga about eleven. After that, I made several more visits. Years later her nephew, the now Reverend Jewell Jones, would often tease us about the old oak tree where we would meet and have our picnics.

The summer I was working at Ben Mott's grocery store. I bought Vi a ring and sent her some money. On Labor Day weekend Vi went to town with her father and some of her siblings. She carried a large paper bag. I have always thought that her mother, Momma Bea, was aware her child was leaving that day, but Vi said nothing to her father. When they reached town and separated to take care of business, Vi caught the bus for Chattanooga. Her siblings said their father never asked about her but just kept singing all the way home. This tells me he knew what was happening.

Early Sunday morning Vi arrived at the bus station. As good fortune would have it, my roommate, Tom Jenkins was there putting some of his family on the bus. He brought Vi to my house and I introduced Vi to others as my wife (although we did not get married until the next day).

In preparation of Vi's arrival, I rented a two-room second-floor apartment. It was small, but we were happy to be there, We had breakfast at my Mother's before we went to our place. Mother loved her right from the start. Vi had been traveling all night and she was tired. So she immediately went to bed and rested. Once she had rested, it was time to prepare Sunday dinner. Everything went well as we looked forward for the next day when we would go to Rossville, Georgia to get married.

We rose early on Labor Day, September 6, 1948 and caught a bus to Georgia. When the minister pronounced us husband and wife, no couple could have been any happier. Over the years I would say that ours was a marriage made in heaven. As I look back, the day of her arrival and the next forty-six years and four months were the dream of my life.

EARLY MARRIAGE AND CHILDREN

In college Vi was a home economics major, but when she first cooked pinto beans, they were hard as parched peanuts. Throughout the years I would tease her with this story time and again. It was not long before she became an excellent cook. As a matter of fact, she became the first of Mama Bea's fifteen children to be allowed to take over the kitchen duties at the farm for breakfast meals. This was saying something.

Our first child was due in January 1949, and we needed more room, so we rented a three-room duplex on Blackford Street a few doors from Mother. While we now had a home, we had no furniture. We got a kerosene heater, a bed, a wood burning stove and a table and chairs for the kitchen. The stove chimney often let loose soot and blue flames would gush from the oil heater, but somehow we made it through the winter.

Our first baby was born January 8, 1949, on Vi's nineteenth birthday. We named her Brenda Valeese. When Brenda was eighteen months old, we had her first picture taken. Vi made a plait (a braid) that curled over her forehead. I still look at this picture and smile.

Unfortunately, our happiness was suddenly tempered due to a tragedy three weeks later, Mary, my sister, lost her life on January 29th. She had gone to the Read House Hotel, where her estranged husband, Ralph O'Neal, worked. Sister went to get money to buy milk for Sandra, their eighteen-month-old daughter. Mary was found the next morning ravaged and strangled but no one was ever arrested for this crime. As far as the Chattanooga police were concerned, solving crimes in the colored community were far from a priority. This was a very sad and trying time for Mother, Vi and me. As little Sandra grew into womanhood, she was the spitting image of my dear Sister. Although she is own person, many times I look at her, think about Sister and wonder what she could have become.

Our second daughter; Deborah L'Tanya, was born in August 1950. In September of '51, our third daughter, Michaellee Moness, was born. That was around the time I had a sudden idea to leave North Carolina Mutual Insurance Company and go back to Nashville with the intention of getting back into college. With three children that dream turned out to be not so practical. So, I returned to Chattanooga and worked from four in the afternoon until midnight as a janitor at Hamilton National Bank. This lasted only a short while and I went back to work at North Carolina Mutual. In 1952 I was promoted to staff manager and our first son, James Jonathan, was born.

The Mapp family, left to right: James Mapp, Viola
Mapp, Michaellee, Toney (kneeling), Angela, Brenda, Ivy,
Jon, Alicia, Deborah–1969. Personal Collection.

HOUSE AND HOME

After Jonathan's birth we moved to larger quarters at 1405 Carroll
Street and later down the block to 1413 Carroll. It was while living at
the latter address that we filed the desegregation suit. Over the next
seven years we had four more children. Angela Maria, born in '55,
Herbert Anthony born in '57, Alicia Victoria born in '59 and Ivanetta
Daphne, born in '60. After the birth of our eighth child Vi told me
in no uncertain terms that that was enough. And I readily agreed.

The housing in our neighborhood was substandard at best – but
typical for lower income Colored housing. Only a few residents
actually owned their homes while most rented from landlords. Most
of the homes were turn of the century wood framed structures, that
were single story and covered with wooden clapboard or tan and red
tarpaper siding that was stamped to resemble brick. All of the houses
had seen better days. We lived in a converted duplex that had two
front doors and a sizable yard with a grass driveway.

Carroll and other side streets of Bushtown were so deteriorated that grass grew through the many cracks in the pavement and along their raggedy edges. After the winter, the city might come through to throw a shovel or two of gravel and some hot tar in new cracks and potholes, but that was the extent of municipal service. All families had empty drums out back where we burned up trash, leaves and rats that regularly found their way into the houses.

With no insulation, our homes could be very cold in wintertime, and very hot in the summer. Where the worn linoleum on the floors had given way to bare wood, getting splinters in your feet was a daily occurrence. The kids would sometimes burn themselves when they got too close to the heater in the front room. The babies slept in same room as Vi and me. while the girls were crowded in two beds in the room next to us. The boys slept in a little hallway across from the bathroom next to the kitchen.

We needed to find a larger home but there were none available in our neighborhood that would accommodate our large family. And we really wanted to move to a better community, so, we went house hunting.

All of this happened during the turmoil with both the student protests downtown and the school desegregation lawsuit in the courts. If you think about it, there couldn't have been a more inopportune time for our family to be going anywhere. The spotlight was on me as head of the NAACP and my name was constantly in the local papers. For us to move into anything but an identical community like the one we were trying to leave seemed a long shot. Living in a community that was mixed with white neighbors seemed an impossibility. But chance and circumstance had other plans.

In the spring of 1962, I was collecting insurance in North Brainerd on Ridgeside Road. I ventured over to the next street and spotted a nice white house with plenty of windows and a carport. It had a very large side and back yard. Most of all, it had a "for sale" sign out front. The address was 514 Terrell Street. I liked it so much that I quit work for the day, went home and got Vi. We drove by and she liked it too, so I called to make arrangements to view the house.

When I called the company, I don't think they recognized the caller as being black. I was told that the real estate agent had left a key on the front porch under a rock, and it would be okay to enter. Vi and I went home to get the children so that they could see it. We all liked the bright inside and especially the smooth oak floors. The kids had never seen floors so shiny and pretty. We all laid down on the floor and took in its coolness. Some of us even took a nap. We were as comfortable as comfortable could be. The house seemed destined for us.

By the time we looked to buy, Terrell Street was occupied by white people only. There were a few Negroes scattered within the North Brainerd community. For instance, my Uncle Willie had a small house a few blocks away. In our efforts to purchase 514 Terrell Street we would experience first-hand the two faces of the white community: one of the expected run-of-the-mill resentment and racial hatred and the other that surprisingly embraced the notion of "live and let live".

As a family, there was no doubt that this was the house for us. Our best hope to purchase the house was to go to the company I was working for to see if we could get them to finance the home for us. They agreed to do so.

The next day I went to the broker's office, owned by two brothers. I told them that I liked the house and I wanted to buy it. I also let them know that financing had already been approved. I immediately realized that they had misunderstood my name when we talked on the phone. Instead of Mapp, my name was listed as Napp. When this was clarified they suddenly recognized that this was the colored fella from the NAACP who was creating all the commotion. One brother looked at me, frowned, turned to his brother and said, "You can have him!" and then left. The other brother nervously asked me, "You don't have to move in right away, do you?" I responded, "No." I was expecting greater pushback. It would be another six years before fair housing laws were passed. But I supposed as I stood there with my financing already approved they figured that a bird in the hand was greater than two in the bush and "a sale was a sale." I quickly signed the papers. The house was legally ours. The price was $9,200.

After the deal was consummated, word soon got out about the purchase. Later I heard that the real estate firm we dealt with was boycotted from selling other houses in North Brainerd.

North Brainerd Days

Right after we moved in, I was constantly in the newspaper as leader of the NAACP. This infuriated my white neighbors. Although Negroes had farmed and lived in the neighborhood almost since the time of slavery, those families were "okay" since there was only a few of them.

There was an instance where the wife of a family living next door to us had been crossing our backyard to hang clothes on the clothesline of the white neighbor on the other side. When we moved in she started going there by way of the street. Vi noticed her change of habit and told the lady she could continue to cross our yard as she had been doing. The woman smiled, and it was easy to see the answer was "thanks but no thanks." Within a few months, they had moved out. Many others on the block became spooked especially when one real estate agent- eager for new sales and commissions - tapped into the century old prejudices and fears that southern whites had for Blacks.

I'll never forget that we moved in June and had planned our vacation for July. Our neighbor on the corner of Terrell and Germantown Road was old Mr. Strong, whose community roots were generations deep. On the day before we moved in, he caught me as I turned the corner onto Terrell Street and asked, "Hey there, you are Mapp, aren't you?" "Yes," I replied, He then went on to say, "You have a number of children, don't you?" To this point I became concerned until he added, "This is good place to raise them. Bring them on out. "I was relieved. I guess I had prejudged him because of his ruddy red appearance, no shirt and overalls. In the end. one could not want for a better neighbor. We decided that we would let him know when we were going to take a vacation and he said, "Go on and enjoy yourselves. I assure you that everything is the same when you get back." And it was. This was a time when we could go up to Booker T. Washington State Park (for coloreds) and leave our front and back doors unlocked and nothing was ever bothered.

It was amazing how quickly white flight in the area took place. Within a few short years, not only Terrell Street but most surrounding blocks had become populated with Black families. I was surprised at how many longtime white residents born in the community and well up in age were willing to leave. One would think that they were settled for life, but they couldn't fathom the idea of being on equal terms with Black neighbors. With exception of a handful, one by one the steady stream of white families moved off Terrell. Those who stayed around were Mr. Strong and his wife, Mrs. Fryars and her son, Mrs. Dudley - whose flowered front yard had an arched entrance with the words "shady nook" on it. There was one other white woman who lived in the tiniest house on the block. The children referred to her as the witch lady due to her closed manner, old age and stooped posture.

I am sure that the residents who remained were wary at first, but they soon found out that Black families were pretty much like any others. When Mr. Strong's house caught fire in the 80's no one gave a second thought as to the color of the young fella up the street named Steve who risked his own life carrying both Mr. Strong and his wife to safety. Like good neighbors, we watched out for one another. And of our white neighbors who didn't participate in the racial exodus, each of them remained on Terrell Street until their death.

Although we now lived in North Brainerd the schools in Chattanooga had yet to desegregate. Our four oldest school-age children went to Orchard Knob Elementary and Jr. High schools in our old neighborhood. Brenda would graduate a few years later at the all-black Riverside High that up until 1960 was the all-White Chattanooga City High School. They built a new "City High" on the Northside of town for the white students: We were fortunate that my mother lived on Highland Park Avenue within walking distance of the children's schools, so I could pick them up from her house after work.

Believe it or not, there were times when I forgot the children. I would park in our driveway and Vi would ask, "Where are the kids?" Then I'd go back across town to fetch them. The daily commute was expensive, and it lasted for years.

COMMUNITY INVOLVEMENT

Vi and I worked as volunteers in many fields, all of which were designed to improve life and living. We were always busy at some task - day and night - and always made ourselves available when called upon to assist in some worthy project. We were filled with ideas that we freely shared. Even with our other activities there was plenty of time for our children.

Our home had one of the largest back yards in the neighborhood. Coupled with our next-door neighbor's yard owned by a black educator Mr. Theodore Foster, the two yards hosted countless games of catch, kickball, hide and seek, basketball and football. With the exception of playgrounds at Sunnyside elementary school about a half mile away, I guess you'd say our yards were the unofficial park in the neighborhood. For not only our kids but for kids through the community. Although Vi and I had eight children, we didn't have the largest family on the block. The Grimes had nine plus a cousin or two and the Russell's had ten children. At one time our single block of 18 houses there were between 40 and 50 children.

We seemed to have made young people from the neighborhood feel welcome. Those were the days when neighbor looked out for neighbor and the kids knew all eyes were on them. Even when our children weren't home, it was and still is a common occurrence - almost fifty years later - for children to knock on our front door and ask can they play in our yard. We always said yes as they understood without saying that there was to be no fighting or bad language. And we were strict in sending them home before it got too late. Vi and I were happy to be a part of a community who trusted us to see after the welfare of their kids.

FAMILY LIFE

Vi and I had eight children and planned most of our activities to include the whole family. We would get into our old car and go places like Fort Oglethorpe (Georgia), Lookout Mountain, Signal Mountain, and Booker T. Washington State Park. This is how we made our fun since we did not have money to go to pay events. Often on Sunday evenings, we would ride around the city up Signal or Lookout mountains and along Missionary Ridge to see the lights below.

Other times we would take picnic baskets to Nickajack dam, sit in the open spaces of grass and look at the boats on the river. The kids had a ball rolling down the hills. On Thanksgiving night we made it a ritual to go downtown to view the Christmas lights.

One of our outings was to Warner Park, the local theme park. One Sunday in 1961 Mrs. Lillian Robinson, her daughter Marie and my family decided to desegregate Warner Park. We entered the park from the East Third Street entrance. When we reached the midway, we were noticed. Shop after shop closed down because of our presence. We came to a shop manned by this young white girl who refused to close. She said, "Shucks, I want to sell my candied apples." We gladly patronized her – The following week there was a long meeting at City Hall to discuss our venture into the park. Not long after, the barriers were dropped, and the park was opened to everyone.

One of our favorite trips was traveling to Viola's family farm in Greenville, Kentucky to spend a couple of days. We used the twelve to fifteen dollars that we would have spent for groceries as gas and expense money. Before the Western Kentucky parkway was finished in the 1980's, the drive on secondary two-way roads would take on average five to six hours. When we traveled our radar was always up. Throughout the fifties and sixties we were cautious as to when and where we would stop for gas or personal relief. Jim Crow was still alive and kicking in many of the rural counties along the way. It was indeed a guessing game to figure out where you would or wouldn't be welcomed. No doubt, even though white merchants and grease monkeys at the filling station weren't always happy to see us…. they nevertheless had no reservation when it came to taking our money.

Many times, depending on the surroundings, it was less of a hassle and safer to just pull off to the side of the road and take a short walk behind a tree in order to relieve ourselves. Vi would never go. Being the southern belle she was, she thought it to be undignified. If I got too tired, I'd find an out of the way parking lot to rest. Fortunately, through all the decades of travel we encountered no serious incidents as this was the price of being colored on the highways and byways.

After our visit, we would often wait until midnight before starting the trip back home. Even so, we would get up to head to work or school the next day. Vi would generally sleep most of the trip both coming and going. I took great pleasure in occasionally glancing her way; admiring her beauty.

Some of our neighbors thought we were well off financially because we took such trips. Little did they know that we were the family of ten that would dine off of one chicken. Each of us had an assigned piece. When we went to Greenville we profited when one weighs our expenses against what we brought back. When we returned home, it was usually with thirty to forty dollars' worth of food items from the farm. And on other trips with all ten of us and our luggage inside, we somehow managed to strap onto the car a stove and another time a self-wringing washing machine. On the highway I am sure we were a sight. But we were a happy sight.

For the kids, the trips were a good learning experience in farm life. They spent many summers in the country with their grandaddy Herbert and Momma Bea. Vi and I would pick them up Labor Day weekend when the Martins had its annual reunion.

Our children still enjoy going to the farm, and now they carry their children and grandchildren there for the same kind of experience. All still have a great time. To have such a respite that costs nothing but cooperation and goodwill has been a real blessing for all the generations who have visited there.

When we traveled it was always an older model car or station wagon. I always carried a rope or wire in the hopes of fixing anything that went wrong or fell off. In all the years we traveled the highways and secondary roads-sometimes without a spare tire- we were fortunate that we were never left completely stranded. Most of the cars we owned already had seventy-five thousand miles or more when we bought them. In 1952 our first car was a 1939 Dodge. Our second was a '42 Ford, that had no heater in it. When I worked during the winter, I would park on a hill facing the east so that the sun shining in would warm up the car and make it warm for the rest of the day. When all ten of us piled into the car as a family, our body heat did the job. We were poor and for the most part, didn't know it. Those were joyous days in spite of hardships. Whatever came down the pike...we were all in it together. That's the magic of family.

Year after year we would hit the road carrying one or more of our kids to some college or university. I would take great pride of affixing to the back and side windows our station wagons the peel and stick decals with the names and logos of the universities they attended. From 1966 to 1984 we had one to three kids in college each year. Their fields of study were varied. We never asked if they wanted to attend but expected them to take both college entrance tests and fill out applications. I guess that without even saying, they surmised that there was a mandate to go beyond high school.

Some would drop by the wayside but would eventually return to finish. When we carried the oldest ones to college, all ten of us were stuffed into the old station wagon. Every nook and cranny was filled with their belongings in and on top of the wagon. Whatever couldn't fit inside was tied down. Off we'd go, even when we were going to two different destinations on the same trip. I guess we looked like the Beverly Hillbillies. The experiences were a lot of fun, and I think all of us looked forward to making such trips each year. As I believe that success is "catchy", I do think that the higher education examples set by our children were responsible for many in the extended family achieving beyond high school.

FAMILY SUPPORT

As I look back, Vi and I did some crazy things and took many chances that may or may not have turned out well given a turn of circumstance. But we were cloaked in faith.... a positive belief that everything would be alright. In hindsight, I shudder at some of the chances we took. We went to NAACP conventions having only money for me as a delegate, yet we carried our four youngest children with us. We bought food at the supermarket to bring to the hotel and dine. Many of our meals came from the exhibit area where they served samples. Now and then other family members were elected delegates and we lived a little easier.

Although there were pressures, there were also areas of support. First was Viola, who stood by my side without complaining. Even though there were many anxious times over our plight she exhibited fearlessness before our children. Every morning taking the children to school, in the most casual way she would tell the kids... "You all be patient while your daddy checks the oil". It was such a ritual that no questions were ever asked. I would go out to the car, lift the hood, check the dipstick and put it back. Then I'd walk around the car and kneel, checking the tire pressure. Through their entire childhood, none of the children ever expected that every morning I was searching for bombs. The children took their cues from Vi's routine and Vi was outwardly that cool and calm.

In the struggle for our rights and freedoms Vi saw the bigger picture. She never once said to me, "Don't go ahead," and she encouraged me to continue. There were times when my confidence was shaken, and she knew that I needed cheering up. And there she was to fit bill.

Much stress was carried by each of us as we both developed ulcers. Vi's ulcers became so bad that in 1970 she had to have emergency surgery. Things were so dire that I was warned we might lose her. But under the skillful hands of surgeon Dr. Edwin Scott, an old Howard High classmate of mine, Vi made it through. She lost a good portion of her stomach, but the successful operation gave her another twenty-five years of life. Once she recovered, Vi was back in the game, more determined than ever. And with the solid support that she always gave, I felt a renewed energy. Everyone knew how special she was. Attorney Avon Williams would tease me about her and say, "How did you get such a beautiful wife?" Then he would add, "I know I look better than you."

Another line of support came from my mother, Mrs. Mattie Hargrove Mapp Davis. Never very emotional, Mother was always quiet and deliberate. When Sister was attacked and killed in 1949, this surely created lifelong anxiety for her, especially after I pushed for desegregation in Chattanooga. Armed only with a sixth-grade education, Mother's depth of understanding of what I and others were trying to accomplish during the rough times was truly remarkable. She was all in favor of progress that especially benefited her grandchildren.

Although she never said it, she knew that there was always a chance her son might share the fate of Medgar Evers or M. L King. She knew that there was a distinct possibility that her remaining child could be taken from her at any time. Mother knew and felt these things, but it never altered her support. This showed her quiet and very real inner strength. In all matters I was involved in that could possibly cause harm to me or mine, Mother never once questioned my judgment or said, "Don't do it." In 1999 at the age of eighty-eight, Mother passed, two months before her eighty-ninth birthday She possessed a great deal of wisdom and a heart full of love. Throughout my entire life she understood her role as my support and soundboard. And when she finally spoke, her wisdom never failed me.

James and Viola Mapp participating in M. L. King Day
march on January 15, 1982. Personal collection.

Although I was in the forefront, I've never been foolish enough
to believe that I could have made it my own. So many nameless and
faceless people quietly contributed in their own way to our shared
victories and progress. Be it by lodging a single vote, contributing a
dime of financial support or the simple act of standing to be counted
meant the world to our struggle.

Vi

In our quest for social justice, at times Vi (Viola) ventured out
on her own. Our oldest daughter was engaged to be married and
Vi wanted her picture to appear in the society pages where no black
person had ever appeared before. Vi contacted the Chattanooga
Times and was successful in convincing them to break down this
racial barrier.

When it came to community service, Vi was highly respected
in both the white and black communities, All of her actions were

based on sound, well-established principles undergirded by fairness and honesty. As the children grew up and left home, she began to take on more community activities alone.

Vi loved working on behalf of young people. For many years in the PTA, she was a local and state leader. She would also become director of the Chattanooga extension of the Baptist Theological Seminary of Nashville.

Viola Martin Mapp. Personal collection

Vi headed the Credentials Committee at the NAACP National Convention for years. Locally she ran the very successful Miss NAACP and Ebony Fashion Fair fundraisers. She participated in the National Baptist Convention and the National Baptist Congress. In Chattanooga, Vi taught skills needed to run a successful Women's Auxiliary program. Soft spoken but firm, Vi was a natural leader who others gladly followed.

When the children came to Chattanooga to visit, they were surprised and entertained at seeing me iron my own shirts because when they lived at home, Vi was the one who kept me and the house in order. Once the kids were gone, Vi hit the road and the domestic roles of our house became open to interpretation. Whether she realized it or not in her own unassuming way, the country girl from tiny Greenville had evolved into a modern-day woman with her own agenda. And I for one couldn't have been more proud to give my full support.

Vi had long been concerned that there was no one managing the Orchard Knob Missionary Baptist church office during the week. So; she volunteered her to set up an official church office, For years she served the church and its members with no pay. As church secretary, Vi showed empathy for many who were troubled and destitute. Folks trusted her. Although some church members were fearful of outsiders who came to the church office for commodities when Vi was alone, she never let this stop her. She attended to the needs of the people as this was her expression of her love for humanity.

Years later the church saw fit to give Vi a salary as she continued to give more than was required - even when she became very sick with cancer.

In '92 Vi received the diagnosis of cancer that the oncologist described as being the easiest to cure. However, this proved not to be the case as she was under treatment for three years. During the first two and half years, Vi would take off from her job only for short periods of time. Because of her illness she later had to give up her church job entirely. A year before she passed, Vi had a very close call with death but was revived and lived for another year. During this time, her sister Ernestine spent a good deal of time with her, giving me some relief. The children all spent some time with her—a week or more at various times during the last year of her life. This was a most meaningful and rewarding year for all of us.

During the Christmas season of 1994, Vi was confined to hospice care at Life Care Nursing Home. I brought her home on Christmas Eve, and we spent Christmas Day together. It was a good Christmas for the most part as we shared a dinner, just the two of us. Immediately after returning to Life Care she had to be hospitalized, and from that time until January 5th, I spent all of my time at the hospital. When the end was near, Vi's youngest brother flew Momma Bea and her

Siblings to Chattanooga on his private plane to say one last goodbye. All Of our children were present when she passed. Just before the end, she looked over and saw her mother, Who said, "Vi, Mama is here." Vi seemed pleased, turned her head and was gone. I never knew there could be such hurt until that moment.

The children all dearly loved their mother, although as a family we weren't the touchy-feely hugging and kissing kind, there was no question there lived a deep and abiding family love at 514 Terrell Street.

My older son and I were talking one day when he said, "You know, Mama never directly told us that she loved us, but we knew." I, myself can't ever recall hearing my own mother say those words outright but there was never a question in my mind that she did. Mother did loosen up by reciprocating with the grandchildren when they told her I love you. That's what grandparents often do. After Vi died, I made conscious decision return their "I love you's" on my own. With each generation I suppose the needs are different and it makes me happy to oblige.

Our children were always very supportive of their mother, and since her death they have given me the same kind of support. Before Vi's death they gave us a trip to Hawaii and a Caribbean cruise. During the years after my seventy-fifth birthday, our children were there to keep me from financial straits, for which I am very appreciative.

At one time I wondered if Vi and I had spent too much time in the struggle. As I look back and watch our children's achievements, it becomes increasingly clear that we did the right thing and they were appreciative of our efforts. They all exhibit a love for human rights and equal opportunity. All have shown competency in whatever endeavors they have undertaken, and for the most part have excelled in spite of obstacles - racial and otherwise - they faced along the way. I believe that having front row seats to the struggles Vi and I faced through the years, made them stronger and more aware of the needs of their fellow man. And most of all, my children have learned that forward progress is a garden that forever needs tending.

111

I am most proud of the manner in which they have reared their children and their evident love of family, Although Vi is no longer with us, for our family, the training and compassion she taught was the tie that binds. She and I were able to share forty-six years and four months before she was taken in 1995. During our time together.... Never was a man so happy as I.

CHAPTER 14

Reflections

LEANING ON THE EVERLASTING ARMS

As I LOOK BACK OVER THE years that Vi and I had spent together, I can't remember us ever stopping to count the cost before we did anything. Instead, we followed our instinct and did what we felt was the right thing to do. Perhaps we were endowed with an extra dose of belief that in the long run, everything was going to be all right. I wonder if sometimes we were purposefully naïve in order not to create doubt or second guess ourselves. We had no crystal ball and I do know that attempting to fully figure out what the consequences of our actions might be could have resulted in wasted time or even worse, missed opportunity.

There is an old saying that the Lord takes care of babies and fools. Well, we certainly weren't babies. I am sure that the same people who have benefited from the many chances we took first thought of us and our actions as fool-hardy. But that didn't bother us in the least. All through life we opted to take the path less traveled. And if there wasn't a path there, we were determined to create one for those brave enough to follow. So, we ventured beyond what was accepted practice of the time and used faith as north, south, east and west on our compass.

In retrospect, we lived a charmed life and were somehow blessed in all that we did. Even when we couldn't fully comprehend the path of whatever journey we were meant to take, we were certain that the blessings from our labor would show up in the end. When we moved from one job to another, one unforgiving task to another, one circumstance to another…it would have been folly to focus on the negative when there was so much to gain.

Such ideals would carry us through our entire marriage. Such ideals allowed us to enter the school desegregation case without fear. Others seemed to worry about us more than we did ourselves and would often give Vi and me their unsolicited advice. We listened politely and then went on about our business. Neither of us dwelled on reprisal. What tomorrow might bring was up to the Almighty. Above all…we kept our senses directed toward the promise our children might one day enjoy. We kept our eyes on the prize. That was the thing that counted most.

James R. and Viola Mapp. Personal collection

We had no reserve of money if the unforeseen happened, but like the sparrow, we toiled but did not worry too much about being provided for. The blessings always came when it seemed that everything was about to fold. There were times when we were about to lose all, including the roof over our heads, but there always came a silver lining to lighten those dark clouds. We never surrendered and kept marching toward goals that we were not sure were within our reach, nor were we sure what the outcome might be. But I suppose this is what faith is all about. And we kept the faith.

We found happiness no matter the burdens. And when we had concerns, for the most part our concerns were for others and especially our children.

Vi and I were able to move through all social levels of society even though we had little to no money. Through conscious effort and self-reliance, we embraced the long-held tradition of Black people in America as we practiced the art of "making do". What we couldn't afford, we made. What we could fix, we fixed. What we could bargain for, we did that too. You'd be surprised at just how far a dollar can stretch if you put your mind to it.

We never considered ourselves poor in any shape, form or fashion. We did not consider that statistically speaking we were barely above or sometimes below what's considered the official poverty line.

People don't realize that so much of "being poor" is a state of mind. Material things come and go and there's so much that we may want, but do we really need it? Tough our family ate more than its share of greens and beans and other low cost but nutritious foods, our children never knew hunger. Vi was a wiz on the sewing machine – mending and making their clothes. Though they were sometimes hand–me–downs, you can be sure that those clothes were always clean. When Easter and other special occasions would come around, Vi would make herself and the girls the most beautiful dresses year after year. Like herself, all of her creations were a wonder.

Those in the white community thought I was receiving financial assistance regularly from my people and that the Mapp's were financially well off. Nothing could have been further from the truth.

At the end of twenty-six years of the desegregation litigation Mr. Dinkins (my attorney at that time) asked me to present a statement about the costs I had incurred throughout the years. The estimate added up to $125,000. The court never ordered that a dime be paid on my behalf. When the litigation was finally dropped, the black community did raise $4,200 for my family. That was it. Hardly anything came from the white community. But Vi and I were okay as we measured our wealth in other ways. As I said…so much of being "poor" is a state of mind.

The worst thing in the world is to fight a battle alone. With Vi and the kids I never felt that way. As we tackled desegregation issues, we had to insulate ourselves within the security of the family. And we protected one another. There were times that I felt I could not divulge to Vi everything that happened to me, and I later found out that she did the same too. And there were many instances that our children encountered situations that would have worried us. It was only years later after they had achieved adulthood did we hear about their tribulations and challenges. I suppose they didn't want us to worry. I was proud to be surrounded by such caring and loyalty that was as strong as my own.

THE FUTURE DEMANDS A CULTURAL CHANGE

Activism comes in many forms, but never by wishing. As freedoms are challenged, vigilance is the watchword and caution is its partner. Our gains won either by chance or circumstance were the result of opportunities created, recognized, or taken advantage of. And once in a while that different kind of person steps up, takes the reigns and says, "if it's to be done, why not me?"

At this time, (2011) nearing almost four centuries of Black people in America, I see for us layers of history. Slavery was the first and most dominant, racial segregation was the second and discrimination based on race is the third. These layers have directly affected the educational and justice systems to this day. These layers have also affected equal access to employment and other opportunities.

Discrimination in all of these areas is becoming more veiled and subtle, making today's problems much less obvious than those in the past. As we become more "Americanized" by taking up the founding fathers' beliefs of individual achievement above all else, I am afraid that our best and brightest are taking the bait. The few Blacks who have "made good" financially and otherwise, seem to have abandoned those like themselves who are not as fortunate. Commitments to our community have weakened as they no longer recognize the necessity of "lifting our own" as we did in the past. Personal greed and enrichment seem to be the new goal as hard-earned lessons from the past are being forgotten.

Overall, it seems that the masses are accepting the notion "What will be will be". And as a people (both white and black) we are resigned to complacency. Even those who are well educated seem to have a lesser sense of history or civic responsibility. Perhaps much of the problem lies in the taking civics courses out of the middle schools.

Brighter Days

Since writing these last passages, *Chance or Circumstance* has allowed me one more time to take a first-hand look at the future of racial relations here in Chattanooga.

In 2012 the local NAACP branch found itself in a bind for leadership as the heir apparent had taken ill and a new leader needed to be elected to finish out the two-year term. I was asked and elected to fill that term. A few months short of my 86th birthday, I began my fourth stint as president of the Chattanooga branch. I am surprised and happy to say that much of the pessimism I had written earlier about had begun to fade. I saw that many in Chattanooga's African American community are now realizing that our goals of equal access in education and the job market are essential if our young people are to survive and thrive. These things must be fought for.

I sensed a renewal and positive attitude to better our condition. This left me with a great faith that many changes could take place in our city.

At 87, Mapp Ends Term as NAACP President

Chattanooga-Hamilton County NAACP President James R. Mapp opens meeting held by the NAACP in this 2013 file photo [photo caption]. Mapp is ending his term as NAACP president at the age of 87. Mapp gave his final speech as president at the NAACP's annual meeting this month. "Even this year Mapp has worked for black people to get better pay and progress in the work-force." *Chattanooga Times Free Press* archives, December 26, 2014.

As the Chattanooga NAACP proceeds in the future, great emphasis should be placed on education, jobs, more inclusion in the areas of criminal justice, housing and economic development. I must say it is a little disheartening that at times history seems to be repeating itself as we tackle some of the same issues that were alive in the 1960s.

The 2010 census listed Chattanooga's African American population at 36 percent with many voters scattered throughout the county. To me, Chattanooga's Black community has yet to realize its true power and leverage its voting strength. I feel the problem is that when it comes to politicians, we are too personality conscious rather than issues oriented. But with education . . . that, too can be overcome.

The title of this book *Chance or Circumstance?* is a reflection of the providential nature of our actions and reactions. What paths we choose to take or not take. As for me, Vi, my children and all others who seek equality and justice and believe in the benefit of full citizenry...I say "bravo" to the spirit and willingness to challenge the powers that be and set them right. In the final analogy two things are true. God helps those who help themselves and no matter how dire the circumstances might be... you can't give up on people. THE END

ABOUT THE AUTHOR

JAMES R. MAPP FIRST LEARNED HOW the system of segregation worked in the south when at the age of 10 he witnessed a white man demand and take his grandpa's farm and horse after hearing they were moving to Chattanooga, Tennessee. The irony was that grandpa did not owe the man anything, but as a black man, he knew that the authorities would not intervene. This incident and others would have a great bearing on Mapp's future endeavors.

Mapp exhibited leadership potential early on while at Howard High School in Chattanooga, Tennessee. He later attended A&I State College (Tennessee State University) where he was elected vice president of the freshman class.

After meeting his future wife, Viola, at Tennessee State, Mapp returned to Chattanooga where he quickly became involved in local issues of discrimination and the injustices suffered by his people. Among other pursuits, he was a leader in the church, cub scouts, PTA and an entrepreneur.

A dedicated family man, James and Viola are parents of 8 children. Their strong bond as a couple helped them to thrive as a family while committing themselves to the fight for equal rights.

President of the local NAACP (National Association for the Advancement of Colored People) for a total of 26 years, James took on the challenge to desegregate Chattanooga's public schools. The court case was said to be the longest running active desegregation suit in the country. He played a major role in opening opportunities for African Americans in jobs, housing, politics, access to public accommodations, and many other areas.

James R. Mapp received many accolades over the years for his community service, leadership, humanitarianism, and civil rights. He was honored by the University of Tennessee at Chattanooga by renaming the James R. Mapp State Office building when it was acquired by UT. Home to physical and occupational therapy majors, the "James R. Mapp Building" fittingly sits on a hill overlooking Martin Luther King, Jr. Boulevard.

In his late 70's Mapp started the pursuit of his goal to capture the history of Chattanooga and race relations. He first learned to use the computer then partnered with Dr. Barbara Medley, professor at UT Chattanooga, to research Chattanooga's history as the backdrop to his memoir. Mapp strongly believed that if not written down, people would soon forget the hard work and sacrifices of the civil rights struggle. He especially wanted to instill racial pride in young people for what African Americans have endured and achieved.

Mapp died on June 19, 2015 after completing his manuscript. Although the Emancipation Proclamation announced the end of slavery on January 1, 1863, Negroes in the south continued to be enslaved for two more years. "Juneteenth" is celebrated by the African American community to commemorate the actual end of slavery in the United States on June 19, 1865.

Juneteenth signaled the end of Mapp's life but his rich legacy lives on.

APPENDICES

The Master's Call

Looking Upon The Fields
And Out Across The Plains
Seeing The Burden Of Injustice
Threatening Freedom's Claim

Bearing Witness To Oppression
Hostilities On Every Hand
The Call Was Made From On High
In Search Of A Mortal Man

One Whose Heart Was Humble
Whose Spirit Was Lowly And Meek
One Who'd Remain Steadfast
For Freedom And Justice That He Seeked

Empowered With The Strength Of Thousands
Yet Gentle As A Lamb
By His Spirit God Called This Servant
James Answered, Here I Am!

Being Led To A Three Day Conference
Decided A Lawsuit Had To Be Filed
To Enforce The Laws Of Desegregation
In Chattanooga's Schools For All!

Unable To Afford A Hotel
In His Car He Slept Those Nights
But By The Dawning Of That Third Day
He Had Accepted The Call To Fight!

Facing Opposition
This Servant Was Undeterred
Filed The Lawsuit In Chattanooga
That Lasted For Twenty Six Years!

His Wife Viola Stood Beside Him
His Rock Of Gibraltershe Became
His Soothing Balm In Gilead
His Comfort When He Was In Pain

Being Threatened And Harrassed
From Chattanooga His Partners Fled
But This Champion Rose To The Occasion
And Remained A True Servant Instead

Protesting Chattanooga's Lunch Counters
Segregated Far Too Long
There Were Those Who Vowed To Join Him
But He Found Himself Alone

Never Wavering In His Commitment
Onward He Marched Alone
God Sent Hundreds Of Howard High Students
Shutting The Business District Down!!

Many Times Denied Employment
His Family Fed By The Black Community Alone
But Despite Those Terrible Hardships
His Fight For Justice Carried On

The Threat Of Death Was Constant
This Servant Refused To Turn Back
For Courage And Determination
Is The Signature Of Mr. James R. Mapp

The Fruits Of His Labor
Did Not Go In Vain
Equality In The Schools Of Chattanooga
Is Now Free For All To Claim

And All Eight Of His Children
Earned Degrees In Higher Education
Lending Their Talents To America's Workforce
Rewarding Their Parents Determination

He's Been Honored With Countless Accolades
Of Which He's Aptly Famed
But The One Most Befitting
TN Clients Services Building Bares His Name

So Bend The Bow Of The Trumpet!
Give It Up For This Tennessee Son
Raise High The Banners Of Valor
In Honor Of What He's Done

Then Sound The Mighty Cymbals!
A Standing Ovation From Your Nation's All
Well Done Thy Faithful Servant
You Answered The Master's Call!

Written By:
Eunice J Goolsby
3/14/2010

Requested By: State Representative Tommie Brown

APPENDIX 2

Excerpt from newspaper article:

Demand Received by School Board
–Negroes Say Urgency of Integration of
Classes is Ignored

Three Negro parents Thursday released the text of a letter they sent to the city school board declaring that they will take legal action if a plan for total integration is not submitted within 24 hours. The text of the letter to the board of education follows:

"Twenty-four hours ago we verbally requested through the superintendent of schools that the board of education submit immediately a plan for total integration of schools.

"To us this is a very grave matter. We expected a reply within 24 hours from the board that would assure us that a plan would be submitted within 10 days.

"You have ignored the urgency of our request just as you have the situation at Orchard Knob School since it became overcrowded in 1947.

"You have not, in our opinion, shown good faith in the implementing of the Supreme Court decision of 1954. The CO asked you to comply in 1954. A committee from the civic league conferred on the matter of implementation of this decision.

"We have asked you to do the same.

"We therefore find it necessary to demand that you submit a plan for total integration within 24 hours. Unless a plan is submitted within this period we shall be forced to take legal action."

The Chattanooga Times archives, February 26, 1960.

APPENDIX 3
Sit-in and Stand-in Participants

February 19, 1960, sit-in students. (Source: *The Chattanooga Times*)

Melvin Davis	Norvel Horton	Phillip Westmoreland
Irene Ricks	Tommy Gordon	Andrew Smith
Frizel Thomas	Ernest Horton	Patricia McGhee
Shirley Jones	Imogene Leslie	Marvin Nicholson
Frankie Hartsfield	James Gaines	Rudolph Graham

Partial list of other students involved in 1960s demonstrations. (Source: *The Chattanooga Times*)

Betty Raines	Melvin Griffin	Joanne Brown
Cortez Greer	Steve Montgomery	Ernestine Shanks
Carrie Wilkerson	Willie Garrett	Ernestine Burgans
Velma Jean Burgans	Elroy Bailey	Doris Johnson
Evelyn Montgomery	Willie (Papa) Ricks	James Bass
Fred Battle	Johnetta Wagner	Geraldine Chambers
JoAnne Humphries	George Cameron	Jackie Wagner
Jackie Jackson	Aaron Woodall	Loretta Cathy
Charles Parks	Joanne Woodall	Billy Edwards
Wanza Lee	Fish McCray	Harrison Berry
Jimmy Cox	Robert Morgan	Edward Sterns
Evon Wilkins	Reginald Days	Ernest Cowan
Steve Montgomery	Imogene Ledford	Mary Ligons
Cynthia Tayler	Mattie Ruffin	Robert Taylor
James Stanley	Charlene Clay	
Wanda Wells	Amelia Allen	

APPENDIX 4

NAACP Chattanooga Branch Presidents

Dates Served	Chattanooga Branch Presidents
1940–1953	Dr. P. A. Stephens, MD—Chartered the Chattanooga NAACP branch April 1940 and served for some thirteen or fourteen years. I had the pleasure of serving under him the last year or two of his administration. Dr. Stephens was short of stature and might be classed as Mr. Five-by-Five. He was very comical with his very husky voice and served well for all his years in office. He was well up in age when he served under Mr. Bryson, the second president.
1953–1954	Mr. W. O. Bryson—Completed his tenure.
1955–1956	Attorney Henry Pearson—Served but did not complete his tenure.
1956	Mrs. Carrie Chapman—Finished the remaining term of Mr. Pearson during 1956. She became the first female to serve as president of the branch.
1957–1958	Mr. William McKinley Kay—Served.
1959–1967	Mr. James R. Mapp—My first tenure in office as president. All of the previous different administrations had prepared me for the task ahead.
1968	Mr. William T. Underwood—Served.

1969–1977	Mr. James R. Mapp—It was during my second tenure in office that I would serve upon the death of the state president Mr. William Vaughn. I would (as first vice president) serve some two and a half years (1975-1978) as president of the Tennessee State Conference of Branches of the NAACP. I would also serve as chairman of the region, which consists of seven southeastern states, for two years.
1978–1982	Mr. George A. Key—It was during his administration that the Chattanooga branch hired our first and only paid staff (a secretary), who was a part-time employee, to man the office. We have not reached that point since.
1982–1983	Mr. Bobby Ward—Served in 1982 after the resignation of Mr. Key. He had a conflict with the executive committee of the branch, which caused the national office to intervene and he stepped down as president. Mr. Ward continues to be a very strong supporter of the branch and national office. Even after he was no longer in office, he could be found attending the national convention, and he might be one of the largest financial contributors to the local branch. He continues to contribute to the state and national NAACP. He challenged the postal service and won his case as our second branch local postmaster.
1983	Mrs. Hannah Martin—Took over as first vice president and served some nine months as president of the branch until a new election was held. I would again begin my final tenure.

1984–1995	James R. Mapp—I would again begin what I thought was my final tenure. Serving six two-year terms.
1996–2004	Mr. Eddie Holmes—Served in the office of president.
2005–2012	Mrs. Valoria Shipman Armstrong—Became president in 2005 at the age of twenty-six.
2013–2014	James R. Mapp—In January 2013 I was inaugurated as president of the Chattanooga Branch of the NAACP. Again, no one was willing to step up to fill the office.
2015–	Dr. Elenora Woods—President of the Chattanooga Branch of the NAACP.

Appendix 5
Documents

March 14, 1961

Raymond B. Witt, Jr., Esq.
Witt, Gaither, Abernathy, Caldwell & Wilson
1234 Volunteer Building
Chattanooga 2, Tennessee

Dear Mr. Witt:

Re: James Jonathan Mapp and Deborah L'Tanya
      Mapp, minors, by James R. Mapp their
      father and next friend, et al.,

                Plaintiffs-Appellees,

          v.

      The Board of Education of the City of
      Chattanooga, Hamilton County, Tennessee,
      et al.,
                Defendants-Appellants.,
                          No. 14,517.

     I have your letters of March 9 and March 10,
indicating the portions of the record which you
intend to print in connection with the second appeal
in the above-entitled case. I understand that your
letter of March 10 replaces your letter of March 9.
It seems clear to us that briefs filed in the district
court do not become a part of the permanent record.
See Rule 11(g), p. 7 of the Rules of the United States
District Court for the Eastern District of Tennessee,
September 1, 1960. We find nothing in the rules of
the Sixth Circuit which indicate that contrary to
practice in all other appellate courts briefs filed
in a lower court are made a part of the record on
appeal.

     I note that in connection with your first appeal
in the Mapp case, No. 14,444, you have printed as a
part of your appendix the briefs filed in the court
below. We consider this to be improper and if you
have any authority for same we would appreciate it
if you would advise us of it.

- Page Two -

Raymond B. Witt, Jr., Esq.   March 14, 1961

I note further that in connection with this
second appeal in the Mapp case, No. 14,517, you
intend, by your letter of March 10, 1961, to print
your brief in support of your desegregation plan.
This we consider improper.

We are suggesting that with respect to the second
appeal there be a joint appendix, as provided by
Rule 16(5) of the Rules of the Sixth Circuit, since
the only thing which we would want to print as an
appendix to our brief and which you have not indicated,
by your letter of March 10, 1961, that you intend to
include in your appendix, is plaintiffs' objections
to defendants' desegregation plan. However, if you
insist upon printing briefs in your appendix we, of
course, would not agree to a joint appendix.

I shall appreciate hearing from you at your
earliest opportunity regarding the suggestion for
a joint appendix.

Yours truly,

Constance Baker Motley
Attorney for Plaintiffs-Appellees

cc: Mr. Carl W. Reuss
     Avon Williams, Esq.

August 29, 1962

Honorable Dean S. Petersen
Chairman of the Board of Education
City Hall
Chattanooga, Tennessee

Dear Sir:

The Chattanooga Branch of the N. A. A. C. P. deplores
and strongly protests the recently reported decision of the
Board of Education to operate a day and a night session at
the Howard School for Junior High students.

It is unthinkable that anyone concerned with the welfare
of youth would subject them, especially the girls, to the
hazards and pitfalls that will be encountered on the streets
after 7:30 at night.

We find it impossible to understand the necessity for this
action particularly since these children were housed in two
schools last year. One of these, the Second District School
having been closed arbitrarily now stands vacant.

We call on you the Board to reconsider your action
immediately in behalf of these students who have already
suffered because of half day sessions and all the other evils
of segregation earlier in their school careers.

In the meantime, we would hope that all parents of
children affected will recognize the dangers involved in

sending their children to school that dismisses at night.

Very truly yours,
Executive Committee
Chattanooga Branch National Association Advancement of Colored People

James R. Mapp
Chairman

CHATTANOOGA BRANCH

National Association for the
Advancement of Colored People

CHATTANOOGA, TENNESSEE

August 10, 1964

Superintendent and Board of Education
1161 W. 40th St.
Chattanooga, Tennessee

Whereas, the school board of the city of Chattanooga has followed a dual education
system for many years because of race and a majority of its units segregated still.
Whereas, As late as the graduating class of 1963, 40% of the Negro graduates have
been listed unemployed, undecided, and unable to attend college (for varied
reasons) as compared with 1% White students falling into these categories.
Whereas, the Negro child has consistently been given inferior education.

Whereas, Continued racial segregation is causing continued overcrowding in predominately Negro schools, predominately White schools have less than capacity loads.
Whereas, The number of teachers (Negro) hired is being reduced because of racial
segregation and do to general segregation practice of the Board.
Whereas, Negro students have less chance of qualifying for jobs after graduation
because of being forced racially to stay in comprehensive high schools and
being virtually eliminated from specialized training especially suited to jobs.
Whereas, the city of Chattanooga has by its Commission been declared an open city.

Whereas, the United States Congress and President have passed a civil rights bill
declaring racial segregation in education ended.
Therefore, We, The Chattanooga Branch of the NAACP, present this resolution calling
for an immediate end to all racial segregation in the school system and calling
for a declaration from the Board of Education of the city of Chattanooga making
known to all citizens that racial segregation in education is no longer practiced.
Therefore, the time has come for Negro children to be given the same opportunity at
quality education to qualify for today's opportunities as White children with
the right to attend the school offering the best in his chosen field regardless
of grade level.
Resolved, that the school board call an emergency session and make an immediate
declaration of policy to the citizens of Chattanooga that, henceforth, there
will be no segregation in the school system starting now, and an order to all
units that they shall in no way, any longer, accept, reject, transfer or assign
on racial grounds.

Submitted by
The Chattanooga Branch National Association for the Advancement of Colored People
Endorsed by its Executive Committee

James R. Mapp, President
Chattanooga Branch NAACP

131

Letter to the Editor

March 13, 2002

The Editors
The Chattanooga Times Free Press
400 E. 11th Street
Chattanooga, TN 37402

Gentlemen:

Simple solutions politically motivated do not solve complex racial problems resulting from years of neglect and deprivation. I was a bit surprised at the Times Editorial on the truancy bill which to me suggest that there is a lack of depth of understanding of the total problem.

REpresentative Brown has a grasp of the complexity and implication of such legislative action having endured the effect of racism and the law when such bills are contrived while Representative Turner has not had to live under resulting actions. Example; the Sheriff calls for more jail space; Representative Turner's truancy bill provides the population; w hile the Hamilton County's "All White" judges deliver primarily Black boys into the criminal justice system and using primarily City policemen are left to do the confrontation (a menu for reducing the Black population, a possible genocidal process).

Truancy should be a local problem with the School Board planning by utilizing Citizens as a TAsk Force to find real solutions.

F or years through letters and press releases I have efforted to arouse the general public by pointing out many of the areas that lend themselves to the problem of truancy: such as, spending millions on Hixson while spending hundreds of thousands on Howard and Brainerd which are older; disrupting attendance shcools two or more times w hile in elementary; demoralizing Black Teachers by placing White Teachers as department heads and lead teachers in predominantly Black schools; lack of hiring of Black Teachers while assigning far too many White Teachers to predominantly Black schools; failing to build and upgrade elementary schools in Black Communities thereby limiting parental participation; and when in this mobile society middle school students transfer to predominantly Black middle schools and announce that they had that basic course last year.

Apparently you have not monitored the more than $200,000,000.00 in bond issues spent or proposed and how little has been spent of these capital funds in Black neighborhoods and how demoralizing it is to Black Students.

Yours truly,

James R. Mapp

James R. Mapp

APPENDIX 6
Mayor's Bi-Racial Committee

Black members:

Mr. Bennie Harris	A local attorney who was vice chairman and who later became the first black city judge.
Mr. Clarence B. Robinson	A local principal who later became a state representative and was also a national figure in the labor movement.
Dr. Major Jones	Pastor of Stanley United Methodist Church who later became president of the Interdenominational Theological Seminary in Atlanta.
Dr. Horace Jerome Traylor	President of Zion College and later vice president of the University of Florida at Miami Dade County.
James R. Mapp	Assistant manager with North Carolina Mutual Insurance Company and president of the Chattanooga branch of the NAACP.

White members:

The Rev. John Bonner	An Episcopal priest who was named chairman.
Mr. William E. Brock	Owner of Brock Candy Company and one of the leaders of the community.
Mr. Williams Raoul	With the Cavalier Corporation and a member of the leadership circle.

Mr. Felix G. Miller   President of Miller Bros.
                               Department Stores.

Mr. Mitchell Crawford   A local attorney.

APPENDIX 7
Proposed Alternate Plan

PROPOSED ALTERNATE PLAN FOR THE DESEGREGATION OF
CHATTANOOGA PUBLIC SCHOOLS

1. Compulsory segregation based upon race is abolished in Chattanooga Public Schools, effective with the school year beginning in September, 1961, and pupils may be admitted to the first grade of elementary schools without regard to race.

2. Effective with the school year beginning in September, 1962, pupils may be admitted to grade two of the elementary schools without regard to race and thereafter in the next higher grade at the beginning of each successive school year until the desegregation plan is effected in all twelve grades.

3. A single system of school zones based upon the location and capacity of school buildings and the latest scholastic census will be established for the admission of pupils to the first grade in 1961 and to other grades thereafter desegregated.

4. During a period of transition to complete application of single zones, children residing in new single zones may continue the practice of attending schools to which they are zoned by existing Board policy by filing a "notice of intent" with the Board of Education prior to August 1, 1961.

5. The privilege of transfer as provided in existing school board policy may be granted students for the following reasons:

    a. When a student would otherwise be required to attend a school where the majority of students in that school or in his class are of a different race.

    b. When in the judgment of the Board, upon the recommendation of the Superintendent it is in the best interest of the student, under Board policy, to transfer him from one school to another.

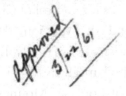

135

APPENDIX 8

Chattanooga: City of Change

THE WORD *CHATTANOOGA* MEANS *"ROCK COMING to a point."* It's an appropriate description of Lookout Mountain, which overlooks the city. From atop Lookout Mountain one can look down onto the Tennessee River as it curves to form a peninsula that looks like a moccasin worn by Native Americans. Between historic Lookout Mountain and the foothills of the Appalachian chain, the lush green valley of Chattanooga reflects its beauty as it has become known as the scenic city of the South.

My adopted hometown has long been a battleground in the struggle for freedom and civil rights. Before the civil war during the Antebellum period, groups of the enslaved called "coffles" were a common sight in the region. Thousands of African men, women and children disembarked from docks along the Tennessee river and were herded like cattle down Browns Ferry road to be distributed to plantations in the deeper south. Coffles were eventually replaced by the more convenient railroad who's many crisscrossing lines made Chattanooga a valued hub of connection and commerce. It was these converging railroad lines that made the occupation of Chattanooga a priority during the Civil war for both the North and the South . . . for whoever controlled them controlled vital supply trains and troop movements throughout the majority of the southern states.

It was during the Civil war campaigns for control of Chattanooga that thousands of emancipated slaves and runaways joined the Union Army. Some became soldiers but most of the newly freed acted as support personnel. They contributed mightily to pivotal Civil war battles in the region: the battles of Lookout Mountain, Signal

Mountain, Chickamauga, Orchard Knob and Missionary Ridge. After the Union defeated the Confederacy and began a prolonged occupation of the region, Chattanooga became a magnet for newly liberated. Encampments called Contraband Camps were established and became a haven for the recent residents. And of those who sought refuge, many would stay and make Chattanooga their permanent home.

Right after the Civil war in 1865 former Confederate soldiers founded the Ku Klux Klan in Pulaski, Tennessee. In 1870 a Tennessee legislative act required separation of white and Negro citizens statewide. These acts set in place the racial temperament of Chattanooga for the next ninety years. Negroes in Chattanooga, like those in the rest of the South, were now subject to what eventually became known as "Jim Crow" laws.

In 1870, after the Civil War and during the era of Reconstruction, Colored men all across the south became eligible to vote. Blacks made up an estimated 42 percent of Chattanooga's total population. This means that they possessed considerable political clout. From 1868 until the early 1900's, Blacks were regularly elected to Chattanooga's governing Board of Aldermen.

Although the Union occupation of Chattanooga had ended in 1877, the promise and influence of Reconstruction had not yet been dismantled. In 1881 there were seven blacks on Chattanooga's twelve person police force. Former slaves appeared in the fire companies, the Board of Education, as justices of the peace, as constables and deputy sheriffs.

Growing Black political strength gained under the protection of Union soldiers rankled local whites. It particularly bothered them that Blacks were on the police force. John E. McGowan, editor of the Chattanooga Times, wrote in 1881, "The negro is utterly and irretrievably spoiled by the badge of authority". In the meantime, Democrats as well as Republicans began to count on black votes. Mr. McGowan lamented in an editorial in 1882 that no party could carry Chattanooga "without toadying to the Negro vote".

In 1883 a concerted effort was made to change the city charter to minimize black political strength. Up until home rule was established in the 1870s, all city charter amendments statewide were made by the Tennessee state legislature. In efforts to eliminate Black office holders, state legislators were asked to repeal the city charter and turn Chattanooga into a "taxing district" to be run by a council of commissioners elected at large and appointed by the Governor. These legislators were told in a petition from Chattanooga's white citizens that "We have no prejudice against the Negroes, but dislike being ruled and ruined by them".

The Chattanooga city charter was not repealed in 1883, but a compromise was reached to provide for a voter's poll tax. The compromise also included special voting registration procedures, a police force under the control of a commission appointed by the Governor, and a reduction in the number of Aldermen to six - five of whom were required to live in their home district.

The Mayor and one Alderman could live anywhere and were elected on an at-large basis. According to Styles Hutchins, a local black lawyer at the time, "The 1883 compromise was aimed at the Negro and nothing else".

The 1883 compromise did not totally eliminate black political influence immediately. Through the Republican party, the Party of Lincoln, blacks managed to elect Aldermen and two state legislators over the next few years. In 1883 registered Black voters actually outnumbered white voters, even though the black population citywide was about 43 percent.

The white power structure in Chattanooga was determined to once-and-for-all squash and altogether eliminate Negro voting power and influence. In 1889, the state stepped in and again amended the city charter to increase the number of voting wards from five to eight, and to arrange by gerrymandering voting districts. This move limited black voting to only three wards.

In 1890, Jim Crow laws were enacted in Tennessee to legalize segregation. This contributed to a greater degree of hardening of attitudes between the races. In 1897 the U.S. Supreme Court's landmark decision of Plessy vs Ferguson upheld the constitutionality of the "separation of races", establishing the "separate but equal" doctrine that was to play out over the next 64 years. All across the South, terrorism against Blacks increased. Chattanooga endured four lynchings between 1885 and 1906. The stage was finally set for a takeover that restored the ideals and idea of white superiority.

Despite adversity, blacks retained an electoral foothold in Chattanooga through the turn of the century, especially in the heavily Republican fourth ward. This presence bothered whites to no end. In 1901 the "Peak bill", still another state legislative revision of the city charter, created a bicameral city government with eight aldermen and 16 councilmen. This eliminated all Black aldermen after 1902 and Blacks retained only two city council seats from the fourth ward. Still, the Chattanooga Times reported that the election of 1902 gave the city "the most representative board of alderman that ever sat in the council chamber of Chattanooga.

At the time, Chattanooga did have quite a number of white Republicans who depended on Black electoral support. In 1905 the Times lamented that the fourth ward was the only Republican holdout in the city, and it could not "be captured from the Negroes by any means". Over the next few years the newspaper continued to express concern about what it saw as political power of black Republicans.

The proposal advanced by white civic leaders to create what became Chattanooga's current form of commission government first surfaced in 1907 and had gained considerable momentum by 1909. It failed to succeed but the delegation did additional gerrymandering to further reduce black voting influence. For this, the *Times* editorial board crowed that "the negroes of Bushtown, Stanleyville and Churchville are about the nearest to disenfranchisement as they could possibly be".

Around 1905, fifty years before the famous Montgomery Bus Boycott, there was civil unrest regarding segregation in public transportation in Chattanooga. Blacks were now required by state legislation to sit in the back of streetcars. Randolph Miller, publisher of the *Blade* newspaper, was a leading advocate of boycotting white owned transit companies.

Black citizens of Nashville and Chattanooga fought back by proposing a competitive public transportation system to be known as the Jitney taxi lines.

To keep the lid on the potentially volatile issue, the Office of the Secretary of State of Tennessee okayed special charters to allow for the creation of this "for coloreds only" transportation line. Jitney taxis would become a main staple of getting around the city for Black citizens. This alternative transportation provided a viable option to Blacks in Jim Crow times and helped "maintain the peace" for more than sixty-five years.

In Chattanooga, the original Jitney Taxi line charter was given to Mr. Carl Angel. It was an immediate success and a boon to the Black community. Upon his death the charter was handed down to his daughter. After her death the carter was transferred once more, but in the late 1960's the charter for the Jitney Line somehow completely vanished from the state records in Nashville. The Jitney taxi line was determined to be an illegal enterprise. Coincidentally, the privately owned Chattanooga bus company had recently been sold to the city and in 1970 the newly formed Chattanooga Area Regional Transportation Authority (known as CARTA) was established with undisputed and total control of the City's public transportation system.

To further neutralize the power of Black Chattanoogans, in 1911 Negro policemen lost their power to arrest and were eventually eliminated totally from the city's police department. It wasn't until 1948 that Black officers were hired again – but with preconditions. Reinstated Negro officers could only arrest those like themselves. A white offender could only be detained until a white officer could make the formal arrest. This policy continued until the early 1960s.

By the mid-1950s Black Chattanoogans attempted serious runs for seats on the city commission. An organization known as the Citizens for General Improvement (CGI) was formed and fielded Douglas Carter to run amidst a large field of white candidates for the four commission posts. This provided an excellent opportunity to elect for the first time a Black commissioner. But a second Black candidate decided to enter the race, thus dividing the Black vote. As a result, each candidate lost by 250 votes. Black Chattanoogans would have to wait another fifteen years to get a seat on the county commission.

After that election, there were other opportunities for Blacks vying for public office in Chattanooga and Hamilton County. Mrs. Phoebe Callier ran for the state legislature in 1959 and lost. In 1966 I ran for the county council and lost. Mr. Lawrence Curry won the office of constable but while in that position, it was said that he had threatened to arrest Commissioner James Bookie Turner, who was white. I am not sure why this transpired, but soon after, the office of constable was abolished by the state legislature. During that time, two other Blacks were elected as justices of the peace. But no sooner had they served their first term, those offices were also abolished.

It was 1971 before there was another serious run for a post on the commission. Local mortician and businessman John P. Franklin mounted a successful campaign for the office of Commissioner of Health and Education. He won handily. But after the election, the office of health was taken away from the position, which left him presiding only over the Chattanooga Board of Education. He served long and well, later becoming vice mayor until 1989.

In 1987 twelve Black Chattanooga residents challenged the use of at-large elections and laws that permitted nonresident property owners to vote in local elections. In 1989 federal judge R. Allen Edgar ruled in the case of *Dr. Tommie F. Brown versus the City of Chattanooga and the State of Tennessee*, that the at-large method of electing members to the commission had been adopted with a "discriminatory purpose that diluted minority voting strength". In other words, at-large elections where all were thrown in the same voting pool unfairly favored the majority white population and were deemed unconstitutional.

Judge Edgar also held that property qualification schemes that allowed non-residents to vote simply because they owned land within the city/county limits, were unconstitutional under the Fourteenth Amendment.

As per the ruling in 1989, the city was divided into nine districts, and as a result, four black councilmen were elected. The tragedy is that twenty years later only two council seats are still occupied by Blacks.

Some might say that "seats were lost" but I believe they were "given away" due to the lethargy of registered Blacks who simply chose not to vote. It never ceases to amaze me how one generation can take for granted all of the heartache and trials the prior generation endured on their behalf.

One election in the not so very distant past there is a district where a white candidate won with 455 votes. Of 3,200 registered voters in that district, some 2,700 were black and only 450 were white.

Such apathy is hard to reconcile especially after the great sacrifices so many have made to secure the vote in the first place. In these modern times, freedom is taken for granted. Black folk don't realize that by choosing not to participates gives others the right to make decisions on their behalf. Only after whatever deed is done, do they cry out and claim foul. Through their lack of participation, the powers-that-be won again. And only after the fact do they question why. It's sad to think that sometimes we can be our own worst enemy and we can't win for losing.

As a result of successfully desegregating the schools in the early 1960s, white flight from the public school system picked up steam. White parents chose to move out to the mostly white county school system. Many enlisted their children in private schools. As a result, by the 1990s public education in Chattanooga became predominately Black. Segregation had taken yet another form.

Mayor Gene Roberts and the city commissioners pushed for consolidation of the city and county schools into one district. Fearing city resources would favor the county schools, the merger was held up in court for two years. In 1996 the two school districts were joined with a white majority population in control.

Progress between the races in Chattanooga has at best been uneven. Those Blacks who now enjoy the benefits and freedoms that others literally gave their blood and lives for are not honored as they should be. Every time we forget, we Black people lose ground to those whose mission is to never sleep until they have total unchallenged dominance.

Are we better off than we were in the days of Jim Crow? I'd say we are. But progress can be such a slippery slope and in no time one can find themselves back in the times of their ancestors.

How do you make people care? How do you make them recognize, honor and old onto that we claim is sacred?

The idea of "who is free" was once defined in the stark terms of black and white. Now, what is considered equal and free comes in many shades of gray. In the final analogy, it's all about control. Control of your destiny, control of my destiny. And to what extent will I allow your destiny to deny me, mine? Must I wait for "chance" --the luck or the draw -- to determine my future? Or will I take an active hand in shaping those "circumstances" that surround me?

I firmly believe that it is up to all Chattanoogans to choose our future. And it is up to us to find the resolve to stick with it. We should own not only our successes, but also our shortcomings and downright failures. We must be honest enough to lay the blame squarely at our feet when due to nobody else . . . we come up short. We must resolve to do better. We must resolve to be better. Chattanooga can only be a city of change – of positive change – if only we remain vigilant and true.

Reference: Official Document:CIV-1-87-388
History of Racism in Chattanooga as Documented by the Federal Court – reported by Tom Griscom: Editor & Publisher *Chattanooga Times Free Press*, October 1999-June 2010.

Appendix 9
Negro/Black/African American "Firsts"

The abundance of "firsts" found in this book are necessary because of the conditions under which we as a people were subjected. The denial of opportunity and indeed denials of Negroes being a part of the human race demands that these "firsts" be very prominent as the reader follows people and events omitted in history books.

The Reverend H. H. Battle	First to serve on the Chattanooga Board of Education.
John P. Franklin	First black to serve in an elected position in Chattanooga city government. First elected as commissioner of health and education (1971). Later became Chattanooga vice mayor.
James Williams	First to serve on the board of the Electric Power System of Chattanooga
Samuel W. Wilkins	First process server in Hamilton County.
Dr. Harry Reynolds	First Superintendent of Chattanooga Schools (in the 1980s).
Ralph Cothran	First to become police chief in Chattanooga (early 1990s)
Richard Thurman	First to become the highest-ranking black, serving as chief of a division, in the Hamilton County Sheriff's Office (1990s)
Mr. Bennie Harris	Became the first Chattanooga city judge

Ernest Varner	First to finish University of Tennessee Chattanooga's Reserve Officer's Training Corps program. Went into military service and remained until retirement
Thomas L. Scott	First in Chattanooga with the designation of CLU (Certified Licensed Underwriter)
Marvin Harris	First to work mail on trains and became first Chattanooga postmaster.
George A. Key	Developed first Negro-owned housing subdivision in the Eastdale area off Greenwood Road, with his son, Charles F. Key (early 1960s).
Dr. Edgar L. Scott	First surgeon to operate in the city-owned Baroness Erlanger Hospital and other hospitals (1963).
Dr. Michael Love	First cardiologist to practice at Erlanger Hospital in Chattanooga (1980).
Dr. Emma Wheeler	First black female physician in Chattanooga (1914). She built a hospital (Walden Hospital) at the corner of East Eighth and Douglas streets. Incidentally, this was a facility for training nurses also. Carver Hospital opened in the 1940s as an adjunct to Erlanger for Negro patients and stood for a number of years on West Ninth Street (Martin Luther King Jr. Boulevard, West).
Marie Acklin	First to serve on the Chattanooga grand jury. First to work in the county clerk's office (driver's licenses).

Dan Windham	First chairman of the Hamilton County Grand Jury (Chattanooga).
James Anderson	First Hamilton County magistrate (Chattanooga).
Yolanda Echols Mitchell	First female selected as magistrate (2007–2011). She also served in the senior position for one year (2007–2008).
Justice Adolph A. Burch	First to serve as a justice on the Tennessee State Supreme Court.
Morris Glenn	First promoted up the ranks to captain in the police department.
Elmer Thomas	First to serve on the City of Chattanooga's Gas Board and also the Plumbing Board. (His entry on the Plumbing Board allowed a number of blacks to get licensed and proceed to become journeymen plumbers—as many as 20 individuals at one time).
Andrew Jackson	First to serve on the Planning Commission of Chattanooga. Has been in business for more than sixty-five years (longer than anyone else on Martin Luther King Jr. Boulevard).
Curtis Collier	First US attorney for the Federal Court of Eastern District of Tennessee.
Ruth W. Brinkley	First African American president/CEO of Memorial Health Care System from 2002 to 2008.
Ardena Garth Hicks	First African American to serve as public defender and the first black to be elected in a county-wide election in the 1990s.

Rheubin M. Taylor	First county attorney and served as a county commissioner.
Willie Haslerig	Honored by President Barack Obama (our first African American president, elected in 2008) as being one of "first" Negroes to serve in the United States Marines, presenting him with a Distinguished Medal of Honor
Walter Tate	First—and only—Negro to be named judge pro tem. First black chairman of the Hamilton County Democratic Party.
David Jennings	First probation officer for the Federal Court of Eastern District of Tennessee.
James L. Jenkins	First paid black scout executive in the United States.
Dr. Hiram Moore	First medical doctor to qualify to practice in Erlanger Hospital. (The requirement was that they have a refresher course every two years. Dr. McIntosh and Dr. Taylor soon qualified.)
Other	• First OB/GYN and first neurologist to practice at Erlanger Hospital in Chattanooga (1980).
	• Chattanooga Post Office:
	o Obbie Dial–First Window Clerk
	o John Bone–First in Supervision
	o Carson Bobo–First in Personnel
	o John McGhee–First in Training
	• Mr. Suttles of Lafayette, Georgia, was the first black to be hired at Chattanooga's Military Cemetery (second largest in the country).

Printed in the United States
by Baker & Taylor Publisher Services